Richie Hughes has written an excellent resource for every believer. Whether we like it or not, our lives are ultimately made up of choices. We must be people who are equipped to choose correctly, and this book helps to train you how to recognize choices, learn from those decisions, and push into everything God has for you.

—JOHN BEVERE
BEST-SELLING AUTHOR OF *THE BAIT OF SATAN*
AND *THE FEAR OF THE LORD*
FOUNDER, MESSENGER INTERNATIONAL

Your life will be the sum of your choices. Finding people who can point you toward wise choices is a game changer. Richie Hughes is one of those guys. His life is a story of making good choices. His wisdom on decision making, passed on in this book, will help you start where you are and go places you never thought you could.

—WILLIAM VANDERBLOEMEN
PRESIDENT, THE VANDERBLOEMEN SEARCH GROUP

Richie Hughes brings wit and wisdom to the reality that your personal choices really do determine your destiny. This book will offer you practical guidance and inspiration toward a better future.

—DAN REILAND
EXECUTIVE PASTOR, 12STONE CHURCH
AUTHOR OF "THE PASTOR'S COACH" BLOG AT INJOY

Richie Hughes has a terrific way with words and the life experience to back those words. His advice is vital in these exciting times. Read, enjoy, absorb, and then apply.

—PAT WILLIAMS
SENIOR VICE PRESIDENT, ORLANDO MAGIC
AUTHOR OF *EXTREME FOCUS*

Life is a series of choices. In *Start Here, Go Anywhere*, my friend Richie Hughes lays out the power of positive choices. I've observed him as a leader make numerous decisions, and he has made the right ones. I am confident this book will instill a deeper level of wisdom regarding life's choices. Not to mention the fact that you couldn't get this extremely valuable information and impartation from a nicer guy.

—ISRAEL HOUGHTON
GRAMMY AWARD–WINNING RECORDING ARTIST

In *Start Here, Go Anywhere*, Richie Hughes captures the essence of choices and their consequences. Out of his own experience as an athlete, father, and accomplished leader, he illuminates the path for others as they face the hard decisions of life. His humility is reflected in his trust in God to guide his steps.

—MARK L. WILLIAMS, DD
SECOND ASSISTANT OVERSEER, CHURCH OF GOD
(CLEVELAND, TN)

From a personal level to a professional level, Richie Hughes is a man of his word. His leadership, humility, consistency, and effectiveness make him one of the greatest leaders I know. I count it an honor to call him a friend. Read this book.

—RICARDO SANCHEZ
DOVE AWARD–WINNING RECORDING ARTIST

I have known Richie Hughes as a leader, coach, and friend. I wish everyone I know could pull up a chair at his table and have at least one conversation. Richie has a wide range of real-world experiences that provide an incredible platform for proven and practical wisdom. *Start Here, Go Anywhere* is the kind of book every leader and parent should read and reread to keep their lives moving in a positive direction.

—REGGIE JOINER
FOUNDER/PRESIDENT, reTHINK GROUP
AND ORANGE CONFERENCES

The great questions are: Who are you? What are you here for? Where are you going? Your past is your history, not your destiny! In *Start Here, Go Anywhere*, you will find the tools you need to get started on the life that you were born to live. Richie Hughes's insight on life will be the very words you need to change your destiny. It is never too late to become what you dreamed!

—REGGIE DABBS
MOTIVATIONAL SPEAKER AND AUTHOR OF *REGGIE*

Richie Hughes is a leader with both spiritual depth and insight. With his lifetime of spiritual leadership he has put his finger on one of the most strategic, yet overlooked principles of life, that is—choices change lives and destinies. You will not only enjoy the refreshing writing style of *Start Here, Go Anywhere*, but you will also learn from the stories and principles that punctuate its pages.

—Dr. Raymond F. Culpepper
General Overseer, Church of God
(Cleveland, TN)

start

here
go anywhere

richie hughes

CHARISMA
HOUSE

Most CHARISMA HOUSE BOOK GROUP products are available at special quantity discounts for bulk purchase for sales promotions, premiums, fundraising, and educational needs. For details, write Charisma House Book Group, 600 Rinehart Road, Lake Mary, Florida 32746, or telephone (407) 333-0600.

START HERE, GO ANYWHERE by Richie Hughes
Published by Charisma House
Charisma Media/Charisma House Book Group
600 Rinehart Road, Lake Mary, Florida 32746
www.charismahouse.com

Unless otherwise noted, all Scripture quotations are from the New King James Version of the Bible. Copyright © 1979, 1980, 1982 by Thomas Nelson, Inc., publishers. Used by permission. All rights reserved.

Scripture quotations marked KJV are from the King James Version of the Bible.

Scripture quotations marked NIV are from the Holy Bible, New International Version. Copyright © 1973, 1978, 1984, International Bible Society. Used by permission.

Scripture quotations marked THE MESSAGE are from *The Message: The Bible in Contemporary English*, copyright © 1993, 1994, 1995, 1996, 2000, 2001, 2002. Used by permission of NavPress Publishing Group.

Cover design by Gearbox Studio
Design Director: Bill Johnson

Visit the author's website at **www.richiehughes.org.**

Library of Congress Cataloging-in-Publication Data
Hughes, Richie.
  Start here, go anywhere / Richie Hughes. -- 1st ed.
      p. cm.
  ISBN 978-1-61638-211-7 (trade paper) -- ISBN 978-1-61638-627-6
(e-book) 1. Christian life. 2. Choice (Psychology)--Religious
aspects--Christianity. I. Title.
  BV4509.5.H834 2011
  248.4--dc23

                                        2011018416

First Edition

11 12 13 14 15 — 9 8 7 6 5 4 3 2 1
Printed in the United States of America

Contents

Foreword

I HAVE KNOWN THE Hughes family for almost thirty years now. I remember Richie when he was a dynamic quarterback for a local high school football team. I also recall the moment during a revival in Cleveland, Tennessee, when the Holy Spirit dramatically touched him and set him on an amazing destiny. That day Richie made a choice to follow the pull he felt deep within his spirit.

I also know of the very difficult time when he lost his beloved sister and brother. The painful struggle his brother endured for many years was the result of the choices he made and the consequences that eventually followed. It was a long and exhausting ordeal, but in the end the Hughes family chose to love unconditionally, pray continually, and believe that God would intervene. I will let Richie tell you the outcome.

As a personal friend and neighbor of Richie's mother and dad, I can tell you that their faith and integrity never wavered as they stood in faith during difficult times. In this book you will discover the power, the pressure, and the provision that are linked to the choices you make. You will also learn that your choices will pave the road for your future. You need to read the "signs" along the way and make the right choices, and never be detoured from the right path. This book is a resource, a road map, to help you find the road of destiny.

—PERRY STONE
FOUNDER, VOICE OF EVANGELISM
CLEVELAND, TN

INTRODUCTION

CONGRATULATIONS, YOU JUST made a choice. Perhaps you were in a bookstore browsing the shelves, and you picked up this book because the cover caught your eye. Or maybe you were having lunch with friends, and one of them told you about this book and suggested you read it. Maybe, just maybe, you randomly picked up this book because it was lying on some cluttered coffee table or nondescript chair and you thought, "Why not?"

For whatever reason, whether you would categorize it as premeditated or by chance, you made a conscious decision to open these pages. And though you might consider this choice small in the litany of decisions you make daily, it is definitely not inconsequential. In fact, this choice, like every other one you make today, has the potential to change your life, for better or worse.

You see, every choice we make, no matter its size or relative importance, has a degree of reward or penalty attached to it. And these choices, stacked up one after another, will affect the kind of life we live. We act—we choose—and ultimately we must live with the consequences. It's the same principle you may have been taught growing up. You reap what you sow. If you make the right choice, you will receive the appropriate reward. If you choose the wrong path, well, you know where that leads.

As God's children, we have free will and the awesome opportunity to make our own choices, but that freedom comes with an incredible responsibility. We must carefully sift through our powerful wants and needs, our conflicting dreams and reality, our complicated hearts and minds to arrive at the right thoughts, feelings, and behaviors.

Some choices are easily made, but others may require hard work, intense research, vulnerable self-reflection, or exhausting discovery. In fact, it may be easier for you to put this book down now than to face the challenging reality that you are responsible for your life path. Yet I urge you to press on. Keep reading. By looking at rich examples from Scripture and life, we will learn from the choices and consequences of others and hone our ability to make the best decisions.

As you read this book, I pray that you will come to realize the decisions you make can have dramatic and long-lasting effects not just on you but also on those around you. Instead of denying those consequences, I hope you will learn to accept the pleasant or painful results of your choices. But please don't stop there. There is good news for those of us who have made bad choices. Our Father is the

God of "in spite of." In spite of our flaws, faults, and failures, God still has a marvelous plan for our lives.

No matter where we start, we can go anywhere. Poor choices do not destroy our future potential to do great things. God loves us so much that He can cover all of these missteps. He gives each of us experiences, challenges, and tests to prove that we can be victorious through His strength. No matter what we've done, we still have hope. God wants to change our future for His glory.

I have learned this truth from experience. I have made many choices, both good and bad, and I have suffered tremendous pain because of my decisions and those of others. Writing this book has been the greatest challenge of my life. I have struggled, believe me, but I finally made the choice to finish what I started. Many days I faced writer's block and truly did not want to continue. Some of the content I will share is excruciatingly painful for me, but my heartfelt intent is to be transparent with you. I believe God allows us to walk through certain experiences so that when the time comes—His perfect time—we can share what we have learned with others. I hope my story helps someone. I hope it helps you.

CHAPTER 1

You Have a Choice

It's choice—not chance—that determines your destiny.[1]
—Jean Nidetch

I LIKE TO WIN. All my life I have believed that if someone is keeping score, I should come in first place. Growing up, I played whatever sport happened to be in season at the time, and I spent the better part of my adult life coaching student athletes. I am very competitive in everything I do, and I realize that's not always a good thing. I battle this part of my personality on a daily basis.

Although I still love to play sports, I can't quite do at forty-five what I used to be able to do at age eighteen. My baseball and football days are over, and my basketball days are numbered. So like many other men my age who strive to be competitive, challenging their bodies and minds in hopes of staying in the game, I play golf.

One day while I was playing golf with a friend, I found myself very frustrated. I was having a series of especially bad breaks. The ball just would not bounce my way. If you know anything about golf, you know it is a sport that requires a high level of skill but gives a low level of success in return. There are just too many uncontrollable factors that can influence the outcome of the game—wind, the speed of the putting green, and the distance of the putt, just to name a few.

Both my friend and I are competitive, and each of us wanted to win badly that day. Of course, he got all the breaks. He hit shots into the trees and yet they would bounce back out into the fairway like magic. Everything was going just right for him. I on the other hand was having no such luck. I made some great shots. They left my club perfectly and actually landed in the fairway, but that's where my good fortune ended.

Partly because the ground was hard and parched from the heat of summer, my shots kept flying down the middle of the fairway and, just as they hit the course, would begin to roll farther and farther away from the mark. I'd end up taking long walks back to the golf cart to follow my errant ball, my frustration increasing with every step.

One shot rolled through the fairway, through the rough, and splashed into the creek. I was annoyed, but I shook it off trying to focus on the next hole. Then, unbelievably, the same thing happened with the next hole. My shot went flying through the air, hitting the fairway beautifully; then it too began to roll off course until it landed in water.

I should have known I was in trouble even before I started the game. The golf course was named after a series of lakes, and indeed there was water everywhere. With each stroke, I became more and more upset, until I was boiling inside. My partner's shots were going into the trees, then coming back out, hitting the cart path, and advancing another fifty yards closer to the green. Why him and not me?

I pressed on, my competitive nature not allowing me to quit or to just enjoy the game and the time I was able to spend with my friend. I didn't care about the beautiful scenery or that I was fortunate enough to not be sitting at my desk wishing I could play a few rounds. None of that mattered because, you see, it was all about the win.

Finally, after battling every force of nature and beyond, I finally got to the green. It was time to make my putt. I was thinking, "OK, let's see the water mess this up!" I told myself that I have perfect form, perfect delivery, and I *will* make the putt. My nice, firm stroke sent the shot toward the hole; then everything seemed to stop as I watched that little white ball roll toward the tiny hole in the middle of the green. I held my breath as my shot rolled into the hole and spun around in the cup. Then the unthinkable happened. It made a U-turn and jumped out of the hole! I was living every golfer's worst nightmare.

I exhaled slowly but then succumbed to the frustration I had been feeling all day. I tossed the putter so far into the woods I might have made the *Guinness Book of World*

Records for throwing a golf club the farthest distance (I'm kidding). My competitive spirit really got the best of me that day. My putter is probably still somewhere in the woods rotting and rusting to this day.

Yet what happened next was probably worse than the horrible tricks my golf balls were playing on me. My friend said, "Richie, the cart girl's watching." I looked up, hoping against hope, but there she was right behind the green. The young woman's cart was full of cold beverages for the golfers, and she had stopped so she wouldn't disturb my friend and me while we made our putts. Unfortunately, she had witnessed the whole thing.

What kind of spectacle had I made of myself? What kind of example was I setting for this young girl or my friend? Everyone at the golf club knew I was in the ministry. What did my behavior reflect about my ability to control my anger? I hadn't thought about any of these things when I was throwing my putter. I was only concerned that I had missed the shot. What had once fueled my success on the playing field had become a stumbling block. My competitive spirit, my desire to win had crossed an invisible line, becoming a weakness instead of a strength.

Have you ever made a choice you regret? We all have at one time or another. Some of our choices are merely embarrassing while others lead to more serious consequences. That day on the golf course I harmed my witness as a believer in Jesus before both my friend and the young woman manning the beverage cart. I could only hope it wouldn't sour her view of Christians in general. Yet I know of others who have struggled with addiction, financial hardship, and even a life-threatening disease because of the decisions they made.

Our lives are shaped by our choices. No matter where we begin, our decisions each day determine where we will end up. We choose to get up every day and go to work or school. We choose whether or not we are going to eat certain foods or exercise. We choose whether we are going to smoke or drink alcohol. We choose what type of sexual encounters we will participate in and with whom. We choose our spouses and our friends. Each of these singular decisions has a consequence that is powerful and lifelong. Even decisions that seem insignificant, like what we eat for lunch, can have a profound impact on our lives and the lives of others.

CHOICES HAVE POWER

In his book *The 21 Most Powerful Minutes of a Leader's Day*, John Maxwell describes a law of momentum that is shaped by our choices. I like his observation so much that I have shared this principle repeatedly and even used it in a Bible study I led for the Atlanta Falcons players. Two years later the players were still putting into practice the lessons learned.

Using the first four kings of Israel as examples, Maxwell explains that we can choose to be momentum fakers, momentum takers, or momentum makers. David and Solomon were the momentum makers. David was a great warrior who conquered territory that gave Israel room to expand, and Solomon oversaw great wealth and built a temple for the Lord to dwell in. Rehoboam, however, was a taker because he obtained everything his predecessors had worked so hard for and disbanded it in just a matter of days. And Saul was what Maxwell calls a faker. He had tremendous potential, but his insecurities kept him from being all he could be; his successors David and Solomon took Israel to the next level.

As I told the players, every day our choices determine what kind of momentum we create. We can be fakers, who have tremendous talent but allow insecurity and doubt to rob us of our effectiveness. We can be takers, who make foolish mistakes or don't give our full effort. Or we can be momentum makers, whose decisions bring great success. This is the kind of person we all should aspire to be. When I presented this concept during the Bible study, I brought cards the players could use to track their progress. Each card had the word *momentum* written in huge letters, and beneath it the three categories were listed: faker, taker, and maker.

The players periodically checked in with me to discuss their growth in becoming momentum makers, and sometimes I'd call and ask, "Hey, what were you today?" The guys knew what I meant, and they were very honest. Some days they'd say, "Rich, I was a taker. I got a penalty because of unsportsmanlike conduct." Or, "I had a bad attitude because I didn't get the ball enough today." Or, "I had a great day. I was an encourager. Our team did well in practice."

Every day when the players made the right choice, their decision affected not only them individually but also those around them, and it helped make the team successful. The same is true for you and me. Our choices have tremendous power to set the course not only of a game but also of a day, a year, even a lifetime.

LESSONS FROM THE GARDEN

I thank God for giving us the freedom to make our own choices. He is powerful enough to force us to do whatever He desires, but He does not function that way. God wants to be in relationship with us, not to have us respond to Him like robots. Where's the fun in that? Whether it's coming from a child, a friend, or a spouse, the words "I love you" aren't nearly as meaningful when they're not said willingly.

The power to make choices is a gift from God, but it is not one we should take lightly. The choices we make either lead us closer to God or pull us further away from Him. Author C. S. Lewis observed, "Every time you make a choice you are turning the central part of you, the part of you that chooses, into something a little different from what it was before. And taking your life as a whole, with all your innumerable choices, all your life long you are slowly turning this central thing either into a heavenly creature or into a hellish creature."[2]

The choices we make determine the people we become. Life would be so much easier if we realized this and lived our lives accordingly. A college student who doesn't study for a test is likely to fail. A man who mistreats his wife shouldn't be surprised when she is indifferent to him. A teenager who breaks curfew shouldn't wonder why his parents don't trust him. We need to heed the words of Galatians 6:7–8: "Do not be deceived, God is not mocked; for whatever a man sows, that he will also reap. For he who sows to his flesh will of the flesh reap corruption, but he who sows to the Spirit will of the Spirit reap everlasting life."

This can be seen from God's earliest dealings with mankind. He gave Adam and Eve a choice—to obey Him and not eat of the tree of the knowledge of good and evil, or to partake of the fruit and suffer the consequences. We all know how that story ended. Adam and Eve's disobedience led to their separation from the intimacy they once had with God. He gave them everything they could possibly need, and He made a point to spend time with them each evening, but their rebellion cost them all of that. As a result of their disobedience, Eve and her descendants would suffer pain in childbirth, and Adam would have to toil to provide food for his family.

We are still reaping the fruit of Adam and Eve's disobedience in the Garden of Eden. Romans 5:12 says, "Through one man sin entered the world, and death through sin, and thus death spread to all men." Adam and Eve probably never thought their decisions would impact their descendants for generations, but that's the tricky thing about consequences. We can't choose them. We'll discuss that point more fully later on, but suffice it to say that we have absolutely no control over the results of our choices, only on the choices themselves. This is why God sets before us one choice that is more important than all the rest.

THE MOST IMPORTANT CHOICE

Christ died for our sins, removing the wall of sin that separated us from the Father, but our disobedience still causes us to live outside God's best. Of the dozens of choices we are faced with every day, the most important one is whether we will choose to follow Christ. Deuteronomy 30:19–20 says, "I have set before you life and death, blessing and cursing; therefore choose life, that both you and your descendants may live; that you may love the LORD your God, that you may obey His voice, and that you may cling to Him, for He is your life and the length of your days."

Although God gives us the freedom to make any choice we desire, His will is that we choose Him and His ways. Why? Because He is our life and the length of our days. Choosing Him is the only way we can spend eternity in God's presence, and He is the ultimate source of peace, joy, fulfillment, and eternal life. He created us, and He knows what we need even better than we do. Jeremiah 29:11 says God has plans to prosper us and not to harm us, plans to give us hope and a future. The best we can do for ourselves will never match God's best for us. It won't even come close.

Sometimes we think we can serve God and still pursue our own ambitions. This too is a recipe for disaster. It is impossible to wholeheartedly love God and be attached to the world. Matthew 6:24 says, "No one can serve two masters; for either he will hate the one and love the other, or else he will be loyal to the one and despise the other." When we attempt to serve two masters, our judgment gets cloudy, and we end up making faulty decisions.

> "Decisions become easier when your will
> to please God outweighs your will to
> please the world."[3] —Anso Coetzer

This is because our choices will always reflect our values. When obeying God is a priority, our choices will reflect that. We will do our best to avoid making decisions that harm our witness or are contrary to God's Word. I regret my actions on the golf course that day, but I know that if I weren't committed to honoring God in all I do, I probably wouldn't have been so embarrassed by my behavior. Nor would I have attempted to avoid making the same mistake the next time I was frustrated by my golf game.

I often think of the admonition of Joshua, whom God chose to lead the children of Israel after Moses's death. When Joshua was nearing the end of his own life, he gathered the Israelites together and prophesied to the people, reminding them of all that God had done for them. God had brought them out of captivity in Egypt, delivered their enemies into their hands in battle, and even gave them land for which they did not labor and cities they did not build.

You'd think that after seeing the Red Sea part and plagues of locusts and frogs descend on the Egyptians, the children of Israel wouldn't want to serve anyone but the Lord. Yet Joshua didn't make any assumptions. After recalling God's goodness, Joshua gave the Israelites a choice that I believe God is extending to you right now. He said, "Choose for yourselves this day whom you will serve, whether the gods which your fathers served that were on the other side of the River, or the gods of the Amorites, in whose land you dwell. But as for me and my house, we will serve the LORD" (Josh. 24:15).

Richie Hughes and his house are committed to serving the Lord, but you have your own choice to make. You may have seen God move mightily in a family member's situation, for someone at your church, or perhaps even in your own life at some time in the past. But you still must choose. You won't be guilty by association. Will you follow God or your own rules? This is the most important choice any of us will ever make.

Choosing Christ will ultimately lead to eternal life and bring God's blessings, but that doesn't mean life will be easy. Not even close. I grew up in a Christian home with parents who loved me and my siblings and taught us to follow the Lord. Yet easy is the last word I would use to describe the journey God allowed us to take. We experienced heartbreak, and we cried many nights as we grappled with choices that would turn our lives upside down.

CHAPTER 2

CHOICES MADE, CONSEQUENCES PAID

*Nobody ever did, or ever will, escape
the consequences of his choices.*[1]
—ALFRED A. MONTAPERT

NOVEMBER 22, 2002, would prove to be one of the most difficult days of my life. It didn't start out that way, though. I woke up early, anxious to get to school, and the day progressed normally. At that time I was coaching a high school basketball team in Gainesville, Georgia, and that day the team had a good practice. Practice after practice, game after game, win or lose I poured my gifts and energy into my fifteen-man team, and I was pleased to see that the young men were making progress.

As was my post-practice routine, I reviewed the team's performance and made plans for our next practice before heading home for the day. Because I didn't have cell phone service in the gym, I checked the voice mail on my office phone before leaving the gym. I can still remember my wife's somewhat-calm but concerned tone, "Richie, you've got to get to the hospital in Chattanooga. Eddie's bad."

What had started out as an average day suddenly began to spin out of control. My heart was beating out of my chest as my worst fears were realized. The thirty-minute flight from suburban Atlanta to Chattanooga, Tennessee, seemed to take hours. I rushed to Erlanger Hospital eager to see my brother, Eddie, but dreading the situation I might find.

But before you can understand what brought me to that fateful day in November, I need to explain a few things about myself and my two siblings. We were all born into a godly family with a rich Christian heritage. I was the oldest; next was my sister, Keri; and my brother, Eddie, was the baby of the family. Our mother was the church organist, our father served on the church council, and together they taught us to value God, family, and hard work.

We were deeply involved in our church, but attending worship services wasn't a chore. In our house going to church was an event; it was fun; we enjoyed it. We were taught the Golden Rule—do unto others as you would have them do unto you—and we learned that our actions brought consequences. We understood that even if we didn't always make the best choices, we could learn from our mistakes. We also learned that we couldn't always choose what circumstances we would find ourselves in. At those times, we would have to do the best we could with what God had given us.

Every parent knows no two children are alike, and this was definitely true in my family. I also believe that the order in which we were born also shaped the choices we would make and the motivations that drove those decisions. I am the typical firstborn. My sister, Keri, was fifteen months younger than me, and she always found a way to enjoy life, no matter what kinds of challenges it brought. My brother, Eddie, who arrived when I was nine years old, was a natural entertainer and typically found himself at the center of attention.

Although we always had a special relationship, Eddie and I couldn't have been more different. While my friends called me conventional, pragmatic, and conscientious, my little brother was larger than life. I followed the rules and always looked before I leaped; Eddie threw caution to the wind.

Eddie had the kind of personality that always lit up the room. Always surrounded by people, calling many his friends, Eddie was full of energy and had a sometimes-unpredictable sense of humor. He was never reticent to be sarcastic or irreverent if it would get a laugh—and often people laughed until they cried when Eddie was around.

A natural performer, Eddie sang in the children's choir and performed in plays. In fact, his passion for singing and acting were a driving force in his life. Our hometown, Cleveland, Tennessee, proved too small for Eddie and his big dreams, and he couldn't wait for the day when he could move away and chase the stars. He wanted so badly to be a success in the entertainment world that he was willing to do anything to achieve his goal. Drawn by the bright lights of the stage, Eddie graduated from high school in 1993, packed his bags, and moved to the Big Apple.

New York City, the mecca for stage actors and entertainers, was a far cry from the sleepy town Eddie had grown up in. So many people to meet, so many things to do, so many places to see—the choices were endless. Upon moving to New York, Eddie got a job working as an entertainer on a tour boat in Manhattan with a long-time friend from our hometown who had previously moved to the city. Eddie loved it. He shared an apartment in Brooklyn with some other performers, but he found it hard to make ends meet. Living in the city was expensive. When my parents visited him at the beginning of the summer, they begged him to return home to the South, where he also could continue to pursue his dream. But Eddie wanted badly to achieve success as an actor or musician.

It's no secret that some people in the entertainment industry lead carnal lives. Nor is it a secret that many actors and musicians identify themselves as homosexuals. Eddie's value of fame led him to do whatever it took to achieve success, even if that meant making destructive choices. He became involved with an MTV crowd that was living a gay lifestyle. It didn't matter to Eddie how he got a record deal or how he got an acting gig in a movie or on Broadway; it was all about accomplishing his goals. Eddie made a choice to do whatever it took to become a success in his field, even if it meant running with the wrong crowd, drinking, taking drugs, and being totally influenced by the lifestyle his friends were leading.

Do you know anyone with an "at all costs" attitude toward success? Perhaps you know someone who has gotten so caught up in sin he can't see a way out. Maybe—just maybe—that person was, or is, you. This isn't the kind of life God desires for you. No one has to live in bondage to self-destructive behavior. Christ came to set the captives free. We can take any burden to the Lord in prayer; He is ready and waiting to bring healing and deliverance.

> "Your choices today will equal your
> lifestyle tomorrow. You determine your
> choices, and your choices determine your
> consequences."[2] —Dr. Ike Reighard

Eddie's finances continued to decline, so at the end of the summer he finally decided to come back south to Atlanta, where I was living. Eddie found work and made many new friends. Unfortunately, the people he met when he moved to Atlanta were no better influences on him than those he left in New York. When I look back, I realize that Eddie was very vulnerable, maybe even needy, at this point in his life. Unfortunately, he didn't reach out to his family, who truly had his best interests at heart. Instead, he turned his trust to other people and lived a life that would ultimately destroy him.

This is so typical of the way the enemy works. Has

Satan ever tried to use this ploy on you? Maybe you are in a relationship right now that you know is not right for you and that God is trying to draw you away from. Take heed and listen to His voice, that tugging on your heart. Let God lead, and give Him complete control. As I am writing this right now, I am praying for every person who reads this, that the stronghold of wrong relationships would be broken off your life or the lives of your loved ones. Don't lose heart that God can change the situation. I am believing with you!

I was teaching and coaching at a Christian school in Marietta, Georgia, when Eddie moved to Atlanta. I was thankful that my brother and I were living in the same town again, and though we were both busy, we tried to hang out as much as possible. One day I asked Eddie to meet me for lunch so I could share some exciting news with him. At the ripe old age of twenty-nine, I had finally met the woman of my dreams, Stephanie. I had asked her to marry me, and to my relief she said yes. I couldn't wait to tell Eddie and ask him to be my best man.

I can remember wondering what his reaction would be. Eddie had known Stephanie for a long time, so I knew he would approve. But I also knew I wouldn't be able to escape a healthy dose of sarcasm from my brother. Stephanie was just eighteen, and I was eleven years her senior. I knew Eddie would do his best to make me squirm. Even though I was the older brother and had spent the better part of my life giving my siblings grief, I squared my shoulders and put on my best smile, knowing I was about to reap what I had sown.

Eddie and I met at a Chinese restaurant. We settled in, and by the time we had ordered, I couldn't hold the news in any longer. So with a big smile on my face, I announced, "Hey, bro, I'm getting married!" At first, Eddie had no immediate reaction. I thought, "OK, he's in shock." After all, I had been single for a long time. I owned my own house, drove a BMW, and had a great job. I was really happy with my life. In fact, I hadn't even been dating much. I mean, what was the point anyway? I was past going out with someone just to go out. If I couldn't see a future with a person, I wasn't going to waste my time or hers. Not to mention the expense.

I waited for Eddie to give some smart response, but nothing came. So I asked, "Eddie, did you hear me? I'm getting married, and I want you to be my best man."

To my surprise, Eddie began to cry. I sat there in disbelief, not sure how to respond. This was definitely not what I had expected, and I was completely unprepared for it. The mood at our table was taking a serious nosedive. I didn't understand; this was so unlike my brother. So I changed tactics. I thought maybe he didn't want to be the best man, so I considered asking him to sing a song instead. Just as I was about to extend an invitation for him to sing at my wedding, Eddie raised his head and looked me dead in the eye. The words he spoke ripped my heart out of my chest, changing my life forever.

"Richie, I'm gay."

CHAPTER 3

HIV, No Way!

Some choices we live not only once but
a thousand times over, remembering
them for the rest of our lives.[1]
—RICHARD BACH

I FELT LIKE SOMEONE had just punched me in the gut. I couldn't believe what I was hearing. My brain just stalled on one word echoing in my thoughts: *gay, gay, gay, gay!* It was just not possible. No way! My little brother couldn't be a homosexual. But looking at his heartsick expression, there was no doubt that he was serious.

Everything within me resisted the truth. I didn't know anyone who would declare himself a homosexual, especially to a guy like me. I mean, I was an athlete and coach, for goodness' sake. I lived in a testosterone jungle. These two worlds could never coexist. You just didn't tell a guy like me that you were gay. God would eventually give me a deep compassion for my brother and others facing similar battles, but at the time I was on an emotional roller coaster. How was I going to deal with this? How were my parents going to deal with this? Eddie had always been attractive and never lacked for dates or girlfriends. He dated the same girl for two years in high school. He wasn't gay, not my brother. That sort of thing happens to other people, not my family!

My parents taught my siblings and me to love all people as Christ does; we were told to love the sinner but not the sin. But Eddie's proclamation was not acceptable. We both knew Scripture was very black and white on the issue of homosexuality. We had read Leviticus 18:22 and 20:13, and 1 Corinthians 6:9-10, which call homosexuality an abomination. We were raised to believe the Bible was the truth, and we knew this was not God's design for human sexuality. What had gone wrong? How could Eddie have strayed so far from his roots?

After he told me, Eddie called home to tell our parents. They were actually visiting friends and got the call at about 2:00 a.m. Eddie met my parents at their house the next day to talk. His demeanor swung rapidly from hysterical to very serious. I know my parents must have been frightened. Eddie's behavior was so out of character.

My parents were shocked to the core when their baby son shared his choice, his lifestyle, his plummet into a dark world. My mother pleaded with him to turn from his decision. It didn't have to be this way. But Eddie was resolute. He had moved so far away from everything he had been taught, and we hadn't even realized it.

For the next few years, Eddie and I struggled in our relationship. He had become the very thing I loathed most on earth. He had allowed things into his life that were detestable to me. How dare he do this! How dare he proclaim this alternative lifestyle and destroy our family. Do I disown him? I couldn't stand what he was doing, but he was my brother. Many nights I would wake up in a cold sweat worrying about where he was and what he was doing. I wrestled with fears about the danger Eddie's actions were putting him in. I feared for his personal safety, and I grieved for the loss of my brother, my heterosexual brother.

Have you ever received news or a report that almost shut you down? Has a loved one ever made you aware of an issue or situation that was so shocking you just didn't know what to say or do? I had no idea that very soon God would intervene in my life and teach me the powerful meaning of unconditional love. Loving others without judgment, genuinely and authentically, is what Christ has called us to do. I had to make a choice. Do I love him? Yes! He agreed to be the best man at my wedding, and I felt so blessed to have him stand with me on one of the most important days of my life. But I have to admit, I struggled with separating my brother—his personhood and who he was to me—from how he was behaving. Did I agree with his choice? Definitely not! But I knew that I loved him despite it all. I won't lie and tell you it was easy, but I came to the place where I realized that above all else Eddie was my brother, my family, and I couldn't turn my back on him.

Loving others without judgment,
genuinely and authentically, is what
Christ has called us to do.

A CRUSHING BLOW

The bomb dropped almost a year later. Stephanie and I had invited two of our closest friends, Cal and Kristi, over for dinner. Cal was the basketball coach at the rival school in our region. While we were extremely competitive when coaching our teams during games, Cal and I found we had a lot in common. So we struck up a friendship and socialized with our wives often.

Our enjoyable evening was interrupted when Eddie showed up unannounced at the door with a guy, his so-called friend. He wanted to talk, and he said it couldn't wait. So I followed them out to the driveway. Eddie seemed nervous, as if he was avoiding something. Finally, after some pointless small talk, the other guy urged, "Tell him, Eddie." It was at that point, while I was standing in my driveway with friends waiting in my dining room, that my brother told me that he was HIV-positive. I looked at Eddie, not wanting to believe him, and then I looked at the other guy standing there almost smug in his attitude. I realized that he was actually enjoying this moment.

Immediately, I thought to myself, "What am I going to do? Do I get irate with my brother? Do I punch his so-called friend?" My world was rocking, my perspective shifting. How could this man be my brother's friend and appear to be so self-satisfied after Eddie's announcement? This was not my definition of friendship. Choices, choices. What do I do?

> "I believe that we are solely responsible for our choices, and we have to accept the consequences of every deed, word, and thought throughout our lifetime."[2] —ELISABETH KÜBLER-ROSS

In the face of this crushing blow, I just shut down. Everything seemed surreal. I really don't remember much about the rest of the night. Eddie left, and I went back inside and finished dinner. When our friends left, Stephanie wanted to know what had happened. She knew something was wrong with me. She kept asking questions until I finally answered. I didn't want to tell her because I felt that would make the nightmare real. My heartbreak became hers. Stephanie and I wept together for all that was lost and all that would never be. Eddie had made a choice that would lead to his death. It was unbelievable, surreal, and so tragic.

Soon after Eddie told us that he was HIV-positive,

my family began researching a world that was virtually unknown to us. Of course, my background in sports took me to the story of Earvin "Magic" Johnson of the Los Angeles Lakers. In the early 1990s, Magic was at the top of his game. He was one of the most accomplished basketball players in the world playing on one of the best teams in the NBA. He had accumulated all types of accolades from Most Valuable Player commendations to World Championship rings. But somewhere along the way to fame and fortune, Magic made a devastating choice. He made a choice to get involved with someone who was carrying the virus. As a result, his life would never be the same.

I'll never forget the press conference on November 7, 1991, when Magic announced to the world that he would have to retire from the Lakers because he had been infected with HIV.[3] America and basketball fans around the globe were shocked at the news. After learning of my brother's diagnosis, I identified so much with Magic's story. I knew he was thriving despite HIV. I thought if Magic could beat it, so could my brother. After all, Eddie was younger. Maybe the cutting-edge medical developments now available to treat HIV could delay or even keep the dreaded virus from advancing into full-blown AIDS. With medication, we hoped that Eddie could live a productive life.

Eddie began taking a battery of antiretroviral drugs that produced serious side effects, including extreme weight gains and losses. His weight would fluctuate as much as forty or fifty pounds within the course of a few months, depending on which medication he was taking. My family spared no expense on my brother's treatment. Our parents were committed to providing the best care for my brother all while trying to keep Eddie's condition secret.

My brother eventually moved from Atlanta back home to Cleveland, Tennessee. Our parents set him up in a nice apartment with everything he needed. My father got him a job, and we hoped that Eddie would get better, live a good life, and that no one would ever know our painful family secret. Life moved on, and we all pretended that the reality of Eddie's condition could be kept at bay. We chose to act as if the situation did not exist.

Shortly after Eddie returned home to Cleveland, our family took a vacation to Florida. I drove down from Atlanta with Stephanie and our two daughters to meet my parents and brother, who were already there. I'll never forget seeing Eddie when we first arrived at the condo. My brother was always into the latest styles, which of course was the total opposite of me. My idea of trendy fashion was a pair of khakis and a golf shirt.

Quick to give a critical analysis whether I wanted it or not, Eddie coolly assessed me from head to toe. No hello, just a thorough evaluation of my hairstyle, clothes, shoes, and so on. For years his greeting to me was something like, "Richie, you need to trim your eyebrows," or, "That belt doesn't go with those shoes." I was used to his criticism and playful sarcasm, and I was ready for it.

I stood in the center of the room and waited patiently while Eddie gave me the once-over. I noticed that my brother had gained considerable weight since I saw him last. Finally, Eddie's critical gaze settled on my hair, where a few gray strands had appeared. He snapped, "Richie, two words: hair color!" Immediately, I fired back, "Eddie, two words: sit-ups!" Everyone erupted with laughter, even Eddie. It was the beginning of an incredible family vacation, and I savored every moment. After all, this might be the last one we would ever take together as a family, and we all knew it.

Still, I questioned my brother's decisions in life. Where had the train come off the tracks? I could not even fathom the emotions Eddie must have been dealing with; I knew only how difficult it was for my parents and me. What were we going to do now in the face of this unwelcome reality? As I struggled to come to terms with questions I knew I might never have answers to, I began to reflect on what specifically leads us to our choices.

CHAPTER 4

What's Behind Our Choices?

*When you have to make a choice
and don't make it, that is in itself a choice.*[1]
—William James

I T WAS MY daughter's tenth birthday. I got up early to do my morning devotional and began my journal entry with the words, "She's ten." As soon as I wrote it, I found myself getting tearful. The sudden surge of emotion caught me completely off guard. Was it the double-digit birthday that got me? Why all of these tears?

I pondered how her life would play out. What circumstances would impact her? Which friends would she surround herself with? What career would she choose? Whom would she marry? Did I really just say that? Marriage? In eight short years my little girl would be eighteen, an adult and as old as her mother was when I asked her to marry me. I couldn't believe how soon my baby might be making such huge life choices.

This reality hit me even harder when my daughter invited me to eat lunch with her at school that day. I quickly adjusted my whole calendar to be there. I knew that the days of her wanting me to have lunch with her at school were numbered, so I seized the moment. At the lunch table, I was amazed at the dialogue between my daughter and her friends. Girls are relational creatures, always looking to connect through conversation and shared experiences. I knew that. I had read the parenting books.

But I was dumbfounded by how mature their conversation was. They were talking about what they were going to do that upcoming weekend, what they should wear for the upcoming talent show, and who was "going out" with whom. They were talking about *boys*. I couldn't believe it. Just where did they think they were "going"? It was just a little too much for me to handle! These ten-year-olds were little ladies. Where was my baby girl? I realized that she had been growing up, and fast, right under my nose.

That day I realized that even at this tender age my daughter's choices are a big deal. Our children make important, life-impacting decisions about themselves, their relationships, and their future every day—at school, church, the dance studio, on the playing field. How can we as parents help our growing children make good choices? I believe first and foremost, we must make the choice to say no.

When your child is a toddler, you do not bat an eye at saying no if you see him or her doing something that could be harmful. Yet so often as that same child approaches adolescence, we parents tend to worry about offending our children. We want them to like us, but let me tell you, confrontation is not always a bad thing. Sometimes it means the difference between temporary unhappiness and a lifetime of pain or hardship.

Even a choice as simple as the seat they choose on the bus or the child they sit next to can have huge implications on the individuals my girls will become. What video games will they see or what songs will they hear because of the person they sit next to? Our children may not realize it yet, but the choices they make impact everyone around them.

"When it snows, you have two choices: shovel or make snow angels."[2] —AUTHOR UNKNOWN

As adults, we make similar but more advanced choices every day. We decide whether to be thankful for another day or angry and impatient for it to end. We choose whether to take the high road with our coworkers at the water cooler or participate in the juicy gossip mill. When we are offended, we choose whether to take it to the Lord or pick up the phone and trash someone else's actions out of hurt and anger. Every day we decide whether to give our employers our best or do just enough to get by. We choose whether to put our children and spouses first or to pursue our own selfish desires.

What motivates a choice? What steps do we take when making a choice? I have watched for years how people assess situations to prepare to make choices, and it has always intrigued me how we go about the process of decision making. What choices did you make as a young person that had a lasting impact on you? Are there any you wish you'd made differently? Are you living with certain consequences of a bad choice? You see, we begin the psychological process of making choices at an early age.

THE ROOT OF OUR CHOICES

Elvis Presley once said, "Values are like fingerprints. Nobody's are the same, but you leave 'em all over everything you do."[3] I believe the king of rock 'n' roll was on to something. What we believe in motivates and guides our choices. The principles, goals, and standards we live by make up our core values. They are the backbone of everything we do. They clarify who we are and what we stand for, and just like our fingerprints, values leave a mark on everything and everyone in our world. They form the foundation upon which we think, feel, and behave, which is the choice process in a nutshell, but we'll get to that in the next chapter.

There is an entire universe of values that influence us, but some of those values are so significant, so vital to us, that despite dramatic changes in society, government, or the people groups around us, they remain unchanged. It's like this, plain and simple: in an ever-changing world, core values are constant. They are the very essence of our existence, and they create the basic blueprint for how we approach life. They shape our goals. They underlie and direct every choice we make in relationships, work, parenting, faith, and more. Our core values provide answers to tough questions and act as light in times of temptation and conflict.

Our core values are shaped by a wide array of sources. During our childhood and even teenage years, our parents are a key influence upon our values, but then as we move out into the world, other sources begin to powerfully shape our values. For example, our church or religious background, our teachers or school, our coaches and teammates, our society, neighbors, friends, and coworkers can all influence our values.

As we mature and develop in both years and experience, our values become more fixed. We begin to determine what is really important to us as individuals. This is why we see people sometimes veer dramatically from the way they were raised. We each choose our core values. The surprising thing is that if you ask most people what their values are, many would not be able to give you an answer.

Our core values are usually so fundamental to our belief system that we barely notice them. God, family, honesty, peace, security, friendship, respect for ourselves and others, responsibility, passion, courage, justice, and service are just a few of the things we tend to value in our lives and in others.

"It's not hard to make decisions when you
know what your values are."[4] —Roy Disney

Do any of your core values match those? I bet if you
sat down and gave it some thought, you could add many
more. Defining your core values will guide you in setting
goals for yourself. If you have trouble thinking of your
core values, consider trying this exercise. If you were to
write your own eulogy, what would you want people to say
about you? That you were honest? A faithful Christian?
Devoted to your family? The central themes that surface
through this exercise are likely your core values.

I participated in an exercise like this not long ago. In
2010, I transitioned out of a church staff position, and as
part of seeking God's perfect will for the next phase for
my family and me, I felt led to make a list of the things
that were nonnegotiable priorities for me, my wife, and
our children. I thought this would be an exhausting exercise, covering weeks, maybe even months. To my surprise,
my list was very short and simple. After hours and hours
of prayer, research, and soul-searching, I discovered this:

1. I want to do something great for God! I want
   my relationship with Him to grow daily, and I
   want Him to mold me into a usable vessel for
   His glory.

2. I deeply desire to be the absolute best husband
   on the planet (at least in my dreams). I want

my marriage to be full of joy daily. Each night Stephanie and I pray, "Lord, let us love each other more tomorrow than we did today."

3. I want my children to know they are absolutely, unequivocally second to nothing else in my earthly life except my wife. I will be available to them 24/7. I will attend every event they participate in if possible. They will know they are the central figure in my life.

4. I want to provide enough for us to live comfortably, but we will not live extravagantly because I am not willing to sacrifice numbers one through three above to generate the necessary income to live that kind of lifestyle.

That's it. Understanding what matters most to me has forced me to make some tough choices. I rarely travel, and if I do, I schedule the trip around my girls' basketball games, concerts, or other activities. I have not sought to network and self-promote, though I have developed numerous master plans and strategies to build corporate and personal brands for other individuals and organizations. I decline numerous invitations that would advance my career, opting instead to spend my time answering my calling. As I write this, I am the assistant fourth grade girls' coach at my daughter's elementary school. That's not quite the NBA coaching path I thought I would follow, but it is perfectly in line with my priorities. I so value my role as a husband and father that I am willing to make sacrifices to guard those relationships. I know numerous people who lay it all on the line for their careers. They travel, network, and promote their businesses or ministries, and even when they are with loved ones, e-mails, text messages, and tweets steal their "face time" with their spouses and children.

I was on that path myself when God gave me a wonderful dose of reality. So many of my friends have wished for more time with their children. They regret missing special events and not being around when their kids needed them. They now long to relive those days, but they can't. So while some may think I am not living up to my potential, I am happy to say this is what works for me. I spend most of my time with the people I love most. I choose to stay close to home and let my family know they are a priority to me.

Defining your core values will make your life much easier. They will give you purpose in life and guide you in setting goals for yourself. They can also give you the confidence and courage to make hard decisions, whether it is regarding your career, family, or spiritual walk. If you want to make the best choices, know what motivates you and make sure those values line up with God's Word.

CHAPTER 5

The Process of Making a Choice

It's sobering to me when I
remember that the choices we
make determine the outcomes we receive.[1]
—Ron Edmondson

Psychologist Alfred Adler argued that every
person's thoughts, feelings, and actions are always
directed toward a goal that individual has con-
structed as the ideal of what he should be, what people
should be, and what his relationships with others should
be.[2] The doctor is correct. Everything we think, feel, or
do is a result of our choice motivation. As I said earlier,
our core values motivate our choices. But what specifically
does the process of making a choice look like?

Here is a simple model that I find useful in illustrating
how the choice process works. Briefly, our thoughts and
beliefs drive our emotions and resulting behavior. In other
words, the thoughts you think in particular circumstances

or situations, whether they are positive or negative, trigger either a pleasant or unpleasant emotional reaction, resulting in behavior that may or may not be in one's own best interest. Think about it like this. Something happens and:

- You have a belief about the situation: *You think.*

- You have an emotional reaction to the belief: *You feel.*

- You make a choice based on your beliefs and emotional reactions: *You act.*

Or picture it like this:

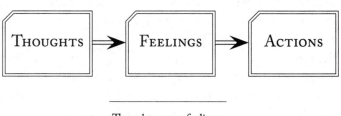

Thoughts cause feelings,
which provoke action.

Everything we feel and everything we do is preceded by a thought. Negative thoughts lead to negative feelings and actions. Positive thoughts lead to positive feelings and actions. It's just that simple. The wrong kinds of thoughts can lead to stressful emotions. The right kinds of thoughts can motivate us to try new things and take risks. The Bible puts it this way, "For as [one] thinks in his heart, so is he" (Prov. 23:7).

Our thoughts control everything we do and how we see the world. Pause for a moment and think about this. Our actions are based solely upon the way *we* think and no one else. People may have some auxiliary impact on our choices, but ultimately we are responsible for our own feelings and actions. We control our paradigm, or the way we interpret things.

I don't believe that we human beings are as compulsive in our behavior as some would have us believe. Has it ever occurred to you that most of our actions are nothing more than *reactions* to a series of thoughts and the resulting feelings that have taken place over the course of time? Believe me when I tell you that your life can be a whole lot more productive and healthy if you can learn to control your thoughts. Remember, no matter what is happening around you, you can choose the way you feel and respond.

It often frustrates me when I hear one of my children say, "She made me do it," or, "You make me sad or angry." Nonsense. I am teaching both of my girls to understand a singular concept. We actively choose to feel the way we do. No one can force us to think or feel a certain way. When someone criticizes or speaks harshly to another person, their anger probably has little or nothing to do with the individual on the receiving end of their tirade. Rather, it likely has everything to do with the state of mind the negative person is in (i.e., what they are thinking and feeling).

The negative individual is projecting his aggression onto a convenient source. Maybe that person thinks the other doesn't like him. Maybe he feels insecure, scared, or has a poor self-image because of thoughts and feelings that are distorted, negative, and downright unhealthy. Whatever the case, the individual chose to respond harshly because of his emotional state. And remember, if someone will speak negatively to you about someone else, he probably won't hesitate to speak badly of you when you are not around.

RENEW YOUR THOUGHTS

So if everything we do begins with a thought, how can we learn the correct way to think? Focus and commitment are the keys. We must become mindful of our thoughts and consider whether they line up with God's Word. The Bible says we are transformed by the renewing of our minds (Rom. 12:2), and this is why our thoughts are such a battleground. The enemy knows that the more our thoughts reflect the truth of God's Word, the more we will become like Christ and walk in His will. When we actively seek God's plan for our lives by developing an intimate relationship with Him through prayer, we position ourselves to make the right choices on a daily basis.

The Bible assures us that God has our best interest at

heart. Jeremiah 29:11 says, "I know what I'm doing. I have it all planned out—plans to take care of you, not abandon you, plans to give you the future you hope for" (The Message). Just about anyone who knows me well knows this is one of my favorite Bible verses. I use it often when I am speaking because I love the promise that the Lord thinks about me and knows what is best for my life. That gives me the faith to trust Him in every decision and to actively seek His will for my life.

When studying Scripture, I like to look up different translations to compare the various wordings. Because I am a pretty simple, straightforward type of guy, I usually enjoy reading *The Message* because it puts the Bible in plain, everyday English. With this particular verse, however, I found the New International Version most interesting. It says, "'For I know the plans I have for you,' declares the Lord, 'plans to prosper you and not to harm you, plans to give you hope and a future.'"

Some of you may be thinking, "OK, Richie, it looks pretty much the same." The two versions are very similar, but I was struck by the word *prosper* in the NIV. Take a look at the first four letters: *pros*. If you are at all like me, when I am faced with a situation and have to make a choice about something, I often will make a list of pros and cons. I am a visual person and have to see things on paper. I need to see that the pros outweigh the cons.

I know God wants all that is good for me and my family (pros), but I also know that we have to do our part in making the right choices so He can bless us in those decisions. We must make our list of pros and cons with spiritual glasses on. God gives us a conscience and expects us to do things that align with His Word. For example, if I have a job opportunity that will promote me to a much better position in the near future, I would not just accept the position without spending some time in prayer about it. If I made my list and the pros were that it would bring more money, a larger home, an ego boost, etc., but the cons were that I would have to compromise on things that were in the best interest of my wife or children, I would have to pass on the offer.

This decision would be based largely around my core values. The fact that something looks attractive and seems to be a blessing doesn't mean it is actually God's best. In fact, it could be the exact opposite. It can be the enemy's ploy to distract us from God's will. This is when wisdom and our morals, ethics, and character (core values) show what we are made of, and these can be demonstrated only through seeking the Holy Spirit's guidance daily.

As you probably know, the word *prosper* means to be successful. It is a verb, an action word. God wants to make us successful. The root word, *success*, means "favorable outcome." Notice that last word *outcome*. Even if you are facing a difficult situation in the present, that doesn't at all mean the final outcome is dire. God's timing is perfect, and He is able to turn anything around for our good. If you will hold on long enough with patience and perseverance, I truly believe you will be able to one day thank God for your valleys, and you will be able to look back and see His hand at work *for your good*.

Too often we equate the word *prosper* with financial success. While that can definitely be part of prosperity, I can think of many more ways I would rather be successful. I want God to make me prosper in my role as a husband, father, and friend. I pray He will bless the works of my hands to make a difference in my community and that I will be faithful with whatever He calls me to do. Success for me is having peace in my home, to love my wife as Christ loved the church, to see my children love and serve the Lord with all of their hearts, for them to find Christian husbands who love them as much as I love my wife.

I can truly say that nowhere on my list of what it means to be successful is a promotion at work, another zero to my paycheck, or one more plaque to hang in my office. I want to provide for my family. I have goals in my work and desire to make a difference in my community, but all of that is done in vain if I have missed nurturing my relationship with my own family, if I fail at being the priest of my own home. Take a few minutes to reflect and ask God if you need to reprioritize any areas in your life. What do you really want the culmination of your choices to reflect when you reach the end of your journey here on earth?

We can rest in the truth that God's plans for us are good. We can place our confidence in Him, knowing

He will never lead us astray. But remember: even when we want to do God's will, it is easy to confuse God's desire for our lives with our own passions and ambition. St. Ignatius of Loyola, founder of the Jesuit order, taught that developing a mind-set of indifference to the choices before us enables us to better distinguish God's will from our own personal desires.[3] Don't become so entrenched in achieving your goals and pursuing your desires that you lose sight of God's purpose for you. Be still, be patient, be in relationship with Him, and He will guide your steps.

CHANGING COURSE

Often I think about Eddie's situation and wonder about his motivation, goals, and choice process. I know that the issue of choice and sexual orientation is a hotly debated topic that has been the focus of much research. Is someone born a homosexual, or does he choose to be a gay? My brother and I had many healthy debates about just that. Eddie believed that he had been born a homosexual. I disagreed. I just didn't see any evidence of it when we were growing up in the same house together.

Eddie had girlfriends, many of whom I knew and had the opportunity to observe as they dated. I remember one especially cute girl my brother dated in high school. Many years later, Eddie told me that holding hands or kissing this young woman never stirred him emotionally.

Then and now, I doubt his declaration. I believe his choice process was distorted by the environment he lived in, the people he surrounded himself with, his drive for fame, and his disconnect from his Creator. As a result, Eddie made a choice to live a homosexual lifestyle. I realize that I may never be able to pinpoint all the factors that led to his choice, but I am convinced that his pursuit of success, as well as drugs and alcohol, were significant factors. My brother made some unfortunate choices during his time here in this world.

I know that some people may disagree with this view, but according to God's Word, which I choose to live by, Eddie's choice to live a homosexual lifestyle was sinful and not ordained by God. (See 1 Corinthians 6:9-10.) Yet a homosexual is no worse in God's eyes than a thief or a man who cheats on his wife. God does not rank sins. We all struggle with areas of weakness, and we all must die daily to the sins of our flesh. Even if we disagree with the lifestyle someone has chosen, the Bible still commands us to love those individuals. Every day I pray that God will help me see people as He sees them and give me a supernatural love for others, the kind of love only Christ can give. I want to be a true disciple of Jesus Christ and honor Him in all I do.

After years of reflecting upon my brother's choices, I have come to believe that his core values prompted him to turn back to God. The seeds planted over a lifetime in our family finally bloomed. Proverbs 22:6 says, "Train up a child in the way he should go, and when he is old he will not depart from it." That certainly proved true for Eddie.

When Eddie hit rock bottom, which for him was having to return to our hometown because he had no money and was growing undeniably weaker, he had to face the reality that he was going to die very soon. At that point, the desperate consequences of his choices could no longer be avoided. God gives all of us free will. We all have the ability to choose even at our own peril. I've often said sinners go to hell by their own choice, not God's choice. Unrepentant sin will send any one of us to hell.

When he was faced with the reality of death, Eddie had nowhere to turn but to the cross. Living back in Tennessee, Eddie began attending the church he grew up in. I can't even describe what it was like to watch him worship the Lord with abandon. To hear the passion in his voice when he talked about what the Lord had delivered him from was exhilarating. Although no one wants to see a loved one endure the kinds of things my brother experienced, in the end Eddie came to love the Lord with all his heart, and he knew he would spend eternity with Him.

Eddie repented of his sin and allowed God to reign in his life. He made the choice to stay at home, secluded and separate from the world, because he knew he couldn't afford to tempt himself and let sin conquer him again. Eddie was weak in his flesh but spiritually astute. I respect him for that choice. Ask yourself, "Could I choose a life of seclusion, isolating myself from everything I loved and felt defined me, in order to remain faithful to God's Word?"

Sadly, Eddie would face the consequences of his lifestyle choices less than a year after that vacation. Unfortunately, no one can escape the consequences of their choices, good or bad.

CHAPTER 6

LESSONS FROM GOD'S WORD

Thoughts shape a man, choices make a
man, and actions reveal a man.[1]
—MARK COLE

W E ARE ALL the product of choices. If Adam and Eve had not made a choice to eat the forbidden fruit, where would the human race be today? If a group of Europeans had not ventured out in search of greater religious freedom and independence, where would America be today? If Martin Luther King Jr. had not shared his dream, what would our relationships with others be like today? If you hadn't chosen your spouse, what kind of life would you be living today? Be careful with that last one!

You've probably heard the saying, "You reap what you sow." Yet that is a truth many of us have a hard time grabbing hold of. In math, one plus one always equals two. In the same way, choices always have consequences.

Choosing to eat that third bowl of ice cream will lead to an upset stomach, and not preparing for a presentation will likely lead to embarrassment. Those consequences are not insurmountable—they can be changed—but there are many choices that can have a devastating consequence. No matter how you slice it, you are free to make your own decisions, but you cannot choose the consequences that come with those choices.

You are free to make your
own decisions, but you cannot
choose the consequences.

Yet so often we seem surprised by the outcomes we experience in life. According to author Russ Lawson, realizing that our actions have consequences is one of the most sobering truths many of us will learn. He writes that whatever we do either affects us or others, and usually both. He uses a great example to illustrate his point. As parents we teach our children not to hit or bite because it can hurt other people. We warn them against touching hot surfaces because we know it can burn them.

> Far too often…we tend to blame someone else for something that is a direct result of our decisions or actions….We often have to face difficult problems in our lives and ask, "Why did God do this to me?" In reality, we are facing consequences that are the result of our own choices and actions, the choices and

actions of others, or maybe even the choices we make with our lifestyle.[2]

Many people are addicted to drugs, alcohol, or nicotine because of a choice they made once to just try it. Countless teenage couples have had their futures forever altered because they went too far one night. Consequences are simply unavoidable, and sadly, many of us have to learn this lesson the hard way.

THE PRICE WE PAY

So how do we respond when faced with the consequences of our choices? Let's begin with what not to do. It's common for us to try to avoid the consequence or hide our guilt. Adam taught us to do just that in Genesis 3:6–13 when he hid from God after eating the forbidden fruit. Adam then multiplied his sin by blaming Eve for his choice. As a result, his descendants, you and I, are still experiencing the consequences of his choice.

This is always the case. Hiding from the consequences of our choices doesn't make them go away. Most of the time it just makes matters worse. For instance, a woman who gets an abortion in order to hide an unintended pregnancy only creates more hurt, both for herself and her unborn baby. Let's learn from Adam's response. We need to accept the consequences of our actions with humility and strength.

Thankfully, we serve a Creator who can wipe the slate

clean and remove our blemishes, giving each of us a brand-new start. But how we respond to God's forgiveness is just as important as knowing He offers it to us. We can accept it and choose to make some changes in our lives, or we can disregard it and continue down a dark path. We see this play out in the lives of Jacob and Esau.

The Bible tells us in Genesis 25–33 that Isaac and Rebekah had twin sons. The younger son, Jacob, is described as a trickster. His name literally means "he who supplants." At birth, Jacob was grabbing the heel of his older brother, Esau, when he came from the womb. As Jacob grew, it became clear that his choice motivation was to have the recognition, power, and blessing of the firstborn child. He thought it unfair that he had not been born first (he thought), and he was jealous of the favor his brother had with their father (he felt). So Jacob plotted a way to achieve his goals (he acted).

Jacob waited until Esau was so famished from working in the fields that he was willing to give anything in return for food and water. When Jacob offered Esau some stew in exchange for his birthright, Esau accepted the deal (Gen. 25:29–34).

I do not believe I have ever eaten a stew so tasty I would be willing to barter my entire future for it, but isn't that how it always is. We don't really take time to think about the consequences. We think about our immediate gratification. In Esau's case, he was thinking about how hungry he was. He wanted something to make him feel better right then. Can you relate to this? I know I sure can.

Jacob, on the other hand, was very aware of the power of his choices. He believed that if he could figure out a way to get Esau to sell him his birthright, he would have a better future. Later, when Isaac was old and his eyesight was failing, Jacob deceived his father into giving him the firstborn blessing. Jacob's mother prepared stew just the way Isaac liked it and helped Jacob cover his smooth skin with hair from a young goat to trick Isaac into thinking he was Esau, who was hairy. Jacob had been gone only a little while when Esau arrived to find that he had been tricked again by his brother (Gen. 27).

It was too late for Esau. He had given away his birthright, and now he'd lost his father's blessing. He could not change the past, and his future would be forever altered. Think about all the generations that have heard about the God of Abraham, Isaac, and Jacob. Had it not been for Jacob's trickery and Esau's impatience, the Lord might have been described as the God of Abraham, Isaac, and Esau.

Wise men and women learn from others' mistakes, and I believe Esau has a lot to teach us. He blamed Jacob for his loss and wanted to kill him to get even, but would murdering Jacob have made things better? Absolutely not! It would have made things much worse. Esau would have not only lost his birthright, but he also would have had the blood of his baby brother on his hands. I understand Esau's anger, but it was aimed at the wrong target. He was doing what so many of us do—blaming someone else when we are frustrated about something we have done.

Now don't get me wrong. Jacob was no saint in this story. He made a selfish and destructive choice for his own personal gain. Although he received what he thought he wanted, it came with its own set of consequences. As a result of his actions, Jacob had to leave his family to flee from his vengeful brother. He lost his peace and security. I imagine Jacob would have changed the past if he could have, but most of the time our actions cannot be undone. This a tough lesson for many of us to learn. Hindsight is always 20/20, and I hope we all learn from these two brothers.

The good news is that God never gives up on us. He is always willing to forgive and forget our mistakes. Jacob didn't get very far before he learned that he had company. God was going with him. The message came in the form of a dream about a ladder that stretched from heaven to earth. The Lord stood above the ladder and said to Jacob:

> Behold, I am with you and will keep you wherever you go, and will bring you back to this land; for I will not leave you until I have done what I have spoken to you.
>
> —Genesis 28:15

Jacob wrestled with God, asking for His forgiveness, and God promised to bless him. No matter how much we mess up, God still loves us and is with us. But the story doesn't end there, and neither do the consequences of Jacob's choices. Sometimes it takes years for the consequences of our actions to rear their ugly heads.

TRICKING THE TRICKSTER

Fast-forward to Jacob's meeting with Rachel. He saw her at a well and fell madly in love with her. After greeting her with a kiss, Jacob decided this was the girl he wanted to marry. I'm not sure he consulted God on this choice, but he offered to work seven years for Rachel's father, Laban, in order to win the right to marry her. Jacob worked hard, pouring all his energy and effort into the task. Under Jacob's leadership, everything Laban owned multiplied and flourished.

At the end of his seven years of labor, Jacob was ready for his reward. It was finally time to marry Rachel. Laban gave his daughter to be married to Jacob. The only problem was that when Jacob woke up the morning after the wedding, the woman next to him was not the bride he expected. Even though Jacob had kept his end of the bargain with Laban, he had been duped. In the morning light, the bride who lay beside him was not his Rachel, but her older sister, Leah.

I have to believe I would have looked at my bride's face, but that's just me. The trickster had been tricked! Laban had sent Leah, the daughter with weak eyes and weaker marriage prospects, to Jacob in marriage. Jacob was angry, but what could he do? Later Laban agreed to give Rachel to him as his bride if he would work another seven years. Imagine, fourteen long years of hard work for the woman of your dreams. All I can say is she must have been a modern-day hottie.

Would you labor patiently for more than a decade for your spouse? I might have done that for my wife, but I am not as confident she would have done that for me. It just kind of hit me one day as I was reading this story: Could Jacob have been reaping what he had sown? He had been doing all the tricking in his earlier years, and now he was duped into marrying a woman he didn't love.

I do not believe God punishes us, but I do believe He gave us free will and permits us to make decisions that may bring unpleasant consequences. I believe He allows certain things to happen to us for our own good. I know I definitely learn best by making my own mistakes, and unfortunately I have made my fair share of them. As we can see in the life of Jacob, even though God forgives us and will protect us, He doesn't always shield us from the fruit of our bad decisions. Sometimes we experience the consequences of our choices years down the road.

I pray that my two daughters marry men who love them and are passionate enough about them to work through any situation. Even now, I pray that the men they marry love the Lord, are great husbands, and wonderful fathers to my grandchildren. You may think it is crazy to have those thoughts and say those prayers when your children are only twelve and ten years old, but it is never too early to begin interceding for our children's future. I pray not only for their future mates but also for their holiness and purity. Every night, I pray aloud so my daughters can hear me. Jacob's problems did not end after he married Rachel and spent another seven years working for Laban. Despite her incredible beauty and a husband who adored her, Rachel was unable to have children. Leah, however, was very fertile and gave birth to many sons and a daughter for Jacob. As a result, Rachel began thinking she was inferior to her sister.

She felt ashamed, angry, and insecure, and she began to resent God. Her thoughts and feelings led her to make a destructive choice. Instead of trusting God, Rachel sent her maidservant, Bilhah, to sleep with her husband in hopes that she would produce a son in her stead. Her plan worked, and Bilhah gave birth to a baby boy. Unfortunately, Rachel was still not satisfied, so she sent Bilhah to Jacob again, and she bore him another son.

While Rachel thought a child conceived and delivered by her maidservant would please her husband and her, it actually caused more strife. You see, some time later the Bible tells us, "God remembered Rachel...and opened her womb" (Gen. 30:22). Finally, Rachel was able to conceive, and she bore Jacob two sons, Joseph and Benjamin. The problem was that Rachel loved her biological sons, especially Joseph, more than the sons Bilhah bore for her. This favoritism would plant seeds of discontent and jealousy among the brothers, eventually leading to Joseph's kidnapping and imprisonment.

What happened? How could Rachel make so many bad choices? Why wasn't she satisfied with the life given to her?

I have asked myself these questions multiple times. It's true that God's grace is sufficient for us, but often our refusal to follow His commandments and our trust in ourselves instead lead us to irrevocably dark places. Let's learn from the story of Jacob. Let's choose to trust God and His timing. Let's choose to accept the circumstances we find ourselves in. Let's choose to focus on the positive, even if we have to bury ourselves in the Bible, reading and reciting Scripture until it becomes woven into the very fabric of our being. Isaiah 26:3 says God will keep him in perfect peace whose mind is stayed on the Lord. God's Word is real. Let it become real to you. You have a choice.

"Our lives are filled with choices, decisions, and forks in the road. When you arrive at these pivotal points in life, remember: the choices we make today affect every future choice down the road."[3] —REP. KEVIN BROOKS

Go With God

In the story of Abraham and Lot we find yet another illustration of the power of choices. Abraham and his nephew Lot were traveling together, and their caravan was huge. They had their families, servants, livestock, and everything they owned, including significant silver and gold.

When Abraham and Lot finally found a good stopping point, they discovered the land was not big enough to support both of their families, animals, and possessions. So as they stood there looking at these two pieces of land, Abraham told Lot to choose which one he'd like to have. Abraham didn't want to fight or argue; he was OK with taking the plot of land Lot didn't choose. Lot thought about the choices before him, but all he could see was the physical beauty of the Jordan valley, which contained the cities of Sodom and Gomorrah. Without much deliberation, Lot quickly selected that land as his home.

His troubles began right away. The people of Sodom and Gomorrah worshiped idols and committed sexual sin so filthy God ultimately felt compelled to take drastic action and wipe them from the earth completely. Lot and his wife had to run for their lives—literally. Sadly, Lot's wife disobeyed the angel's instructions and looked back to the sinful city she had grown accustomed to. As a result she was turned into a pillar of salt (Gen. 19:26). Lot's choice to live in a plush, comfortable land came with a great price.

So what does an Old Testament Bible story have to say about your life and the way you choose to live it? Was Lot really such a bad guy? Was he any worse than you or me? Those are good questions that don't have easy answers. In 2 Peter 2:7, Scripture describes Lot as righteous, yet he had made a poor choice. God didn't abandon Lot; after all, He sent angels to rescue him and his family before destroying

Sodom and Gomorrah. But Lot's decisions cost him his home and even his wife.

There is one figure in this story that I'd like us to give closer attention. Long before Lot looked at the Jordan valley and saw that it was lush and well watered, perfect for his animals to graze and crops to flourish, Abraham made a choice that would transform his life and ours.

In Genesis 12, the Bible says God spoke to a man named Abram and told him to leave his father's house and go to a country He would show him. God promised Abram that He would bless him and make his name great, that He would bless those who blessed him and curse those who cursed him, and that through Abram all the families of the earth would be blessed. Can you imagine getting a call like that? God didn't offer Abram a map or a guarantee that there wouldn't be difficulty along the way. He just said go, and the Bible says Abram "departed as the Lord had spoken to him" (Gen. 12:4).

Throughout the Bible it is well documented that God honored His promise to Abram. He ultimately changed Abram's name to Abraham, which means "father of many nations," and He did indeed bless those who blessed his descendants and curse those who persecuted them. Abraham was a godly man who made a choice to live a life pleasing to God. By doing that, God took great pleasure in blessing not only Abraham but also all of his descendants as well. That's you and me. As Christians, we are children of Abraham and heirs to this awesome promise

(Gal. 3:29). We are still reaping the benefits of one man's obedience.

Oh, that I could make a simple choice that had that type of positive, lasting impact on all who come after me. How about you? What choices can you make today that will positively impact generations to come? That is an incredibly powerful thought. Let's take a lesson from Abraham and commit to following God's Word and being led by His Spirit. We can avoid poor choices and the painful consequences they bring.

CHAPTER 7

In the Valley of Decision

If you think in negative terms you will get negative results. If you think in positive terms you will achieve positive results. That is the simple fact... of an astonishing law of prosperity and success.[1]

—Norman Vincent Peale

W HY DO SOME people make better choices than others? Why does one person consistently lack money while another individual with the same level of income manages to save enough to buy a house? Why does one child finish high school and college while the other drops out and refuses to keep a job? Why do some young women float from one destructive relationship to another even though they keep reaping the same disastrous results?

Choices are personal. They reflect a complex host of our thoughts and feelings, and they are a product of our life experiences as well as our own innate and learned tendencies.

Each decision we make illuminates our character, our desires, and even our insecurities. Yet as the only creatures made in the image of God, we have been given an awesome gift. Instead of simply reflecting our own personalities, we have the opportunity to imitate God's character in our thinking, feelings, and behavior, and thus in the choices we make. God loves our uniqueness—He gave it to us—but He wants us to look more and more like Him. Why?

No matter what the world says or how things sometimes seem, there is only one path to true success. As we saw in the previous chapter, when we align our beliefs and behavior with God's Word and allow ourselves to be led by the Holy Spirit, we position ourselves to make the kinds of choices that bring good consequences.

Because the choice process is so personal, I asked some friends of mine to tell their stories. Although you may not be able to relate to their specific experiences, the principles they share can apply to anyone. First stop, the pitcher's mound.

FOCUS, CONVICTION, KNOWLEDGE

Former Atlanta Braves pitcher John Smoltz spent more than two decades in Major League Baseball. During that time, he was selected eight times to play in the All-Star Game and received the Cy Young Award, which honors the best pitchers in the League. John is also the only pitcher in Major League history to top both 200 wins and 150 saves.[2]

John has played in hundreds of games, and every time he stood on the pitcher's mound he had a choice to make. Fastball? Slider? Curve ball? In one of our many conversations I asked John how he determined which pitch to throw. This is what he told me in his own words:

> If I stand on the mound, and I think about the worst thing that could happen and don't fully commit to the pitch, then the worst thing will happen. But if I'm convinced that a certain pitch is best, even if the batter gets a hit, it was the best choice, because I made it with conviction. I didn't waffle around. I saw it through. After every pitch, every choice, I can reevaluate and determine whether or not I want to throw the same pitch or do something else entirely.
>
> Accumulating information and surrounding myself with the right data is also essential for me to make the right choices. If I were to just go out there and blindly make decisions, then I might as well flip coins.
>
> During my career, I have sometimes found myself on the mound making poor choices, being inconsistent. I soon discovered that my choices were suspect if my mind was not in it, if my commitment was not there, and if I didn't pay attention to the signs. I can relate my choice process to James 1:8 and its theme of double-mindedness. You cannot serve two gods or two masters. If a man doesn't serve God and seeks the things of this world, he will be weak.
>
> I relate that scripture to baseball like this. When I stand on the mound across from the player at bat, I can't be double-minded in my thinking. I can't be

carrying thoughts or worries about fleshly things around in my head. I can't be thinking about the result of the pitch before it happens or my stats or the money I may make if I can throw a shutout and keep the other team from scoring. Doublemindedness doesn't create the peace and serenity I need to get in the zone and throw the pitch. I have to focus and lock in on the hitter.

I'm in a battle. That's why it's important for me to have a certain mental toughness and an ability to see the signs that are coming my way so I can make adjustments. My catcher will tell me things he sees from his vantage point. The manager will tell me what he sees, and my pitching coach will throw in his two cents. While I'm trying to focus on the pitch at hand, I'll have four views to juggle: mine, the catcher's, the manager's, and the pitching coach's. Which pitch will I choose to throw?

I have to consider their input but then really focus on myself, what's inside me, and make a choice. The people around me don't have to throw the pitch and experience the consequences. They're only making suggestions. I'm the only one who knows how I feel, how my arm is aching, and how much strength I have left in me. The bottom line is this: when I cross the white lines, no matter what my catcher says, no matter what my bull pen wants me to do, I have to be committed to executing a certain pitch. And if I'm not, if I'm worried about all kinds of other things, then I'll never be the best pitcher I could be.[3]

"Accumulating information and surrounding
myself with the right data is essential for
me to make the right choices. If I just go
out there and blindly make decisions, then I
might as well flip coins." —JOHN SMOLTZ

Did you notice the principles John expressed here? Focus, commitment, and knowledge are critical to his choice process. He gathers input from individuals who have a different vantage point than he does; then he weighs that data against his own sense about which choice he should make. Ultimately, he has to tune out everything except his choice and commit to the pitch. If he allowed himself to get distracted or to let others choose for him, he never would have become the pitcher God blessed him to be. John says the same principles apply in his walk of faith.

If the choices I'm making are serving the world, then, yes, I've gained the world, but I've lost Him. The bad choices I make each day and on the pitcher's mound—and even the decisions that aren't necessarily bad but don't bring much of a return—are usually indicators of some kind of lack—a lack of information, lack of structure, lack of discipline, or some other lack. So the more information I have, the more structured my thinking and feeling, the more disciplined my environment, the better choices I make.

The same thing applies to my walk with Christ. It is a constant, daily grind to stay disciplined, structured, and all the other things I need to be a great pitcher. But this is what brings joy, and having peace and joy is really what the Christian walk is all about. I now know that there's no joy in the things of this world. Sure, there's happiness, but that's a peripheral feeling that comes along with money, fame, and material things. They aren't central to who we are and who God is calling us to be. Joy is central. It's the greatest peace.

If I live my life to serve Christ, then I've lost nothing. If the Bible, which I believe to be the truth, is the guide, and I choose to live away from its guidance, then I've lost everything. Nothing could replace the love God has for us. Christ dying on the cross for us supersedes anything that we could possibly attain materially. It takes a lifetime of walking daily in God's presence to realize that truth, but our choices either lead us closer to Him or take us farther away.[4]

Do you see what I mean? We may not be professional baseball players choosing week after week which pitch to throw, but we all must choose whom we will serve, what we allow to motivate our choices, and whether or not we will put God first. The path to success truly is the same for all of us—follow Christ! We may not be able to measure our success by the size of our bank accounts or the number of material things we have obtained, but God's economy is not based on those things. Romans 14:17 says God's kingdom is righteousness, peace, and joy in the Holy Spirit. That's real living.

TRUST GOD'S PLAN

For many people, especially Christians, singer and song-writer Mac Powell has found success. He fronts the Grammy– and Dove Award–winning Christian rock band Third Day, which is known for songs such as "Revelation" and "Cry Out to Jesus." Third Day is one of the most celebrated bands in Christian music today, and their music can be heard around the world, but their road to success in the music industry has been marked with both blessing and sacrifice. When I sat down and talked with Mac, he described their journey as a series of choices that sprang from one very important decision they made as a band.

> People can look at what we do, what we have done, and think we've won the lottery in a way. Third Day has been very fortunate and blessed by God to be where we are in the music world, both Christian and mainstream. But in order to have success, there has been great sacrifice. As a band, we were willing to make choices, to take chances that would require sacrifice, because we were so strongly committed to what God had called each of us to do.
>
> I think today it's easy for people to get caught in the trap of making decisions based on finances. Some of my friends even are working jobs that they don't love, doing things they don't want to do, all for the buck. Decisions should be based on God's call on your life, following your passions, what He has put into your heart, because there lies great fulfillment and peace even if it requires sacrifice. Whether you

are an athlete, a musician, a teacher, a scientist, whatever, choose your passion.

But let me caution you! Often what people love to do in life is not what they were meant to do. Many people may think they are great singers or great athletes, but they do not possess the real talent to be successful in that arena. Know that if God calls you to do something, not only will He give you a passion for it, but He also will equip you for the task and confirm His calling through the words and actions of other people. I really have a heart for telling people to pursue their passions and dreams, and not to base their life choices on finances. As a band, we made the decision to follow our dreams, sacrificing financial security. Sometimes we have to let go of something to let God do His work. God has so many options for us that we can't even see, so we have to trust that He has a plan.

We took a chance and followed God's call, and our sacrifice has been rewarded tenfold. Not just in monetary means but in joy, peace, fulfillment, and thousands of lives coming to salvation. We have been able to communicate God's overwhelming love for His creation to so many people who might never have had the chance to hear the gospel. God has used our music to support and encourage so many Christians as they walk this journey of life.

The journey can be straight; it can be curvy; it can lead you upward and downward. It requires us to make many choices, but not every one is life-changing. Not every decision we make is between right and wrong. Sometimes it's just a choice, and we don't need to obsess over it. We just need to choose. For example, when I'm driving in the car with my kids, and I ask them if they want to eat at Burger King or McDonald's, neither of those choices is necessarily the wrong one. It's just a simple choice. They have to pick one or the other. We make these kinds of choices every day.

Don't get me wrong. There are definitely rights and wrongs in life. I'm not talking about those kinds of choices. But whether you pick one fast-food joint over another, or go down the right fork in the road instead of the left, God is still in control. God is the One who opens and shuts doors in our lives. Our task is to pursue Him and be willing to let go of things that stand in the way of His call on our lives.

One instance in particular when I knew that in spite of me, the band, our manager, everyone, God was in complete control and His will was done in His timing was during the recording of *City on a Hill*. Third Day had recorded the title cut for the album, but the producer wanted me to sing vocals on another song with the group Caedmon's Call. My management company insisted that I not sing on the song because we ran the risk of my voice being overplayed. Their concern was that if I were to sing vocals on a song that was not Third Day's, then Third Day's music might not get as much airtime because radio DJs wouldn't want to play two songs in a row that featured my voice.

I agreed with the management company, but because of my friendship with the producer of the album and the tug on my heart, I decided to go against my managers and ask for forgiveness instead of permission. It was a hard decision, but I chose to sing vocals on the track "God of Wonders," and the rest is history! The bottom line is, I made a decision that on the surface was not a good business decision because it might have taken a song away from Third Day, but it turned out to be a great ministry decision. The song exposed many people to Third Day's music who might not have listened to us before because they enjoyed "God of Wonders." This choice won us many new fans and sold a lot of records.[5]

"Whether you are an athlete, a musician, a teacher, a scientist, whatever, choose your passion." —MAC POWELL

Mac and the rest of the members of Third Day were committed to following God's call on their lives, even if that meant making sacrifices. I pray the same can be said of you and me. When we choose to follow Christ, we won't always know where the journey will lead. Mac didn't know how his singing on "God of Wonders" would affect Third Day's radio airplay. Even when we walk in obedience to God, we won't be able to choose the outcome. But we can rest in the fact that God plans to bring us to an "expected end" (Jer. 29:11, KJV). In other words, we can trust Him because even if we don't know where we're going, He does.

If you're anything like me, I bet you wish you could peek a little down the road to see what plans God might be unfolding. Hindsight is 20/20, but foresight isn't so clear. There have been many times when I've tried to follow God's leading and still managed to fail miserably. Of course, there have been plenty of times when I didn't try so hard to discern His will. Thankfully, our mistakes don't count us out. God is bigger than our faults and failures, and no matter how hard we've fallen, He's there to help us make a comeback.

CHAPTER 8

I Am God of ... "In Spite Of"

Many of us crucify ourselves between two thieves—
regret for the past and fear of the future.[1]

—Fulton Oursler

H E WAS A great worker. Always on time, he gave a great effort and had an excellent attitude, but drinking a couple of beers after work to take the edge off turned into an addiction that cost him his job.

She was a star student headed to the university on a full scholarship. But she got in the car one day with a guy who'd had one too many, and now she's paralyzed from the neck down.

He was a great guy with lots of friends, but a little online chatting grew into replies to pop-ups for hot girls. Now his inbox is cluttered with ads asking, "Want to take a peek?" And his addiction to pornography has cost him everything.

She was a model wife, committing her whole life to

her family. She cooked and cleaned and was the family taxicab, running the children to their events all over town. But through a little thing called Facebook, she discovered an old boyfriend from high school one night, and online chatting worked its way into an innocent cup of coffee and then another meeting here and there. You know the rest of the story.

We all know people like the ones above. You may even be struggling with issues of your own. Praise God, the truth of the matter is that God can still use those people, and He can still use you. God has a purpose for all of us, and He loves those who have failed to walk in His ways as much as He does those who sit on the front row at church and volunteer in outreach ministries.

You may have made a disastrous choice that yielded dire consequences. Yet God still has an incredible plan for you. Nothing is over until God says it's over. Nothing is finished until He says it's done.

This truth hit me powerfully one Thanksgiving morning when I was lying in bed feeling especially thankful for some great things God had done in my life. As I lay there in the quiet before daylight came, I felt more blessed than I could ever deserve to be, and I just wanted to spend a few moments in worship. Soon I felt something in my spirit, and my heart sang with the knowledge that the Lord was impressing on me something He wanted me to know.

I was excited that God was speaking to me, but I had no idea how His words would radically change my thinking.

I'll never forget the words that have been burned into my heart. He said, *"Richie, I am God of 'in spite of.'"*

Now believe me, I don't get inspiration like this very often. I'm a pretty simple guy, not some great prophet or preacher who hears from God on a consistent basis. At that time, I was the executive pastor at a megachurch in the Atlanta area. I wasn't the preacher. I wasn't the teacher. I was running the business operations, researching and analyzing ways to make our church and its various ministries operate more efficiently. So a revelation like the one I received that Thanksgiving was completely unexpected.

I wasn't sure what God meant by His statement, so I pressed Him. "OK, God. What does that mean?"

Again, I heard these words in my spirit. *"I'm God of 'in spite of.' In spite of your fear, failures, or faults; in spite of your faith or lack thereof; in spite of what you believe to be the end, the final verdict—I am God of 'in spite of.'"*

I have to admit, I was astounded. I knew without a shadow of doubt that God had given me this message for a purpose, one much greater than I realized at the time. But I couldn't help but wonder why He gave it to me. What could I learn from it? After many months of prayer, study, and reflection, I came to the conclusion that the word God gave me that morning was not for me only but also for others. And it had everything to do with my journey toward understanding choices and consequences.

I began to comprehend that although our fears, failures, faults, and faithlessness do significantly impact our choices and their consequences, God is in control of it all. He is God and always will be. He is the author and finisher of our faith, of our lives. He is God in spite of everything that hinders or distracts us. He just is.

IN SPITE OF FEAR

Over time, God began to unpack this message for me. I began to see the common experiences that cause people to think God will no longer use them or, worse, that He no longer loves them. I praise God that even our bad choices don't disqualify us from being used. Samson allowed his lust for Delilah to cost him his God-given strength, but God still used him to defeat thousands of Philistines (Judg. 16). No matter what we have done, God's perfect plan for us can still be executed to some degree.

Of all the issues that can hinder us from moving forward after missing the mark, fear is undoubtedly among the biggest obstacles. I believe with all my heart that God does not want His children to be enslaved by fear, but let's get one thing straight. Fear is inevitable; we cannot escape it. However, the way we choose to understand it and react to it is not.

If I were to ask you to catalog your fears, you could probably come up with a pretty exhaustive list. Most people could. Spiders, heights, being alone, losing a loved one, going broke, aging, being diagnosed with cancer, and dying are just a few of the more universal fears we all face.

If you were to say to me, "I'm not afraid of anything,"

I would have to politely tell you that you are in a state of denial. You see, according to psychologists and medical professionals, fear is actually hardwired into our brains. It serves as a mechanism for our self-preservation. We can now pinpoint certain regions of the brain that are in charge of managing different fear responses. Fear can also activate the brain, causing it to send messages to the body to freeze or prepare for a fight.[2]

Think about it like this. If you were driving down the street and another car suddenly pulled in front of you, your brain would instantly respond. Fear activates your body and mind to deal with the very real threat that is before you. You might thump on your car horn, slam on your brakes, or swerve out of the way to avoid a collision. You might even go for broke and do all three. Regardless of your response, your fear just helped to save your life.

This is *productive* fear. Being aware of the dangers around you and respecting the threat they might pose to you or your family are healthy. There is another type of fear, however, that can paralyze or even destroy us. This is an *unproductive* fear. Being so afraid of what others might think of us that we isolate ourselves from relationships is unproductive and unhealthy. Fearing that no one will ever love us or that we cannot give love in return is unproductive, even downright destructive. We can become so afraid of facing reality or dealing with emotional pain that we turn to drugs, alcohol, or sex to escape. Rather than enhancing our lives by protecting us from real danger, unproductive fears chip away at our potential to have healthy, happy lives.

In fact, unproductive fear can become so overwhelming that it controls our every thought, feeling, and action. It can so consume us that we miss out on the joy and abundance God has purposed for our lives. Fear is a double-edged sword; it can save or it can destroy.

"We choose what attitudes we have right now.
And it's a continuing choice." —JOHN MAXWELL[3]

What if David had been afraid to face Goliath? What if fear had wrapped itself around his soul, keeping David from fulfilling his God-given purpose? Fortunately, we don't have to answer that question because David did show great courage and met the giant on the field of battle. But what made the difference?

First Samuel 17:37 says, "Moreover David said, 'The LORD, who delivered me from the paw of the lion and from the paw of the bear, He will deliver me from the hand of this Philistine.'" The difference was David's trust in God. Even in his short seventeen years, he already had experienced God's faithfulness time and again. He knew God would be with him; David knew without a doubt that he wouldn't be alone in the fight.

David was so connected to God that he didn't question the outcome; he followed God's hand. As a result, I don't believe that David was ever afraid that he would fail. It never entered his mind. His trust was so great, he never faltered. Can you imagine having a faith that strong and unwavering?

I think it's important that we understand we should not be fearful. We shouldn't be afraid to venture out and trust God about anything in our lives. He is sovereign and in complete control of every situation we find ourselves in. We can have the same confidence in God that David had.

You Can Be Like David

When faced with a terrifying situation, fear can seem like the only viable option, but it is possible to safeguard the role of productive fear in your life while protecting yourself from the disparaging effects of unproductive fear. The first step is to understand just what has you gripped with fear.

We often act on our fears without thinking. Simply taking the time to search yourself and identify what is really making you afraid could go an incredibly long way toward diminishing the strength of unproductive fear. Consider how you react in certain situations. Do you push away important people in your life, refusing to get too close just when the relationship was going well? Do you sabotage healthy relationships because you are afraid of rejection? Is that productive or unproductive fear? Identifying unproductive fear can help you pinpoint the trigger and choose a more productive way to deal with that fear or insecurity.

Next, you must face your fear. You must confront it; stare it in the face, refusing to turn away no matter how uncomfortable you feel. You can't avoid the truth. Facing your fears will give you power over the irrational unproductive fears that plague you. Remember, you have control over your thoughts, feelings, and actions. You do not have to be a slave to fear. If you change your perspective, you can change your life.

As the father of two daughters, it pains me to see the pressure young girls face to have the perfect body, whatever that is. Most rational people know a real person would be hard-pressed to resemble a picture that has been digitally enhanced. Yet as bad as they are, the typical body image issues young women struggle with these days pale in comparison with a condition called body dysmorphic disorder.

Individuals suffering from this condition don't just fret over not having the perfect body or complexion. They believe they are extraordinarily ugly, even though they look as normal as you or me. Some of them are actually quite attractive. Yet they see themselves completely differently. In some cases, their self-perception becomes so warped they remain in their homes, refusing to go to work or engage in social activities because they fear what people will think of their appearance.[4]

There's nothing actually wrong with their appearance; the only problem is their self-perception. A limited number of people suffer from body dysmorphic disorder, but many people suffer with a wrong view of themselves. It may not keep them closed up in their houses, but it can keep them from fulfilling God's purpose for their lives. This almost happened to young Gideon, but God intervened.

Gideon felt completely unqualified to deliver Israel from the oppression of the Midianites, and he told the Lord as much. "So he said to Him, 'O my Lord, how can I save Israel? Indeed my clan is the weakest in Manasseh, and I am the least in my father's house'" (Judg. 6:15). But the Lord didn't see him as weak and small; He saw Gideon as a mighty man of valor. When Gideon's view of himself began to match God's, he experienced the victory the Lord promised—and with an army of just three hundred, no less! Getting a new perspective truly can make all the difference.

The third way to prevent fear from taking control of your life is to substitute faith for your unproductive fears. There are many things to be afraid of in life, but we can be assured that God is not the author of those fears. Second Timothy 1:7 says, "God has not given us a spirit of fear, but of power and love and of a sound mind." You don't have to be afraid. You can live in the fullness and promise of His Word.

Nothing in life or death can separate us from the love of God. Romans 8:37–39 tells us, "We are more than conquerors through Him who loved us. For I am persuaded that neither death nor life, nor angels nor principalities nor powers, nor things present nor things to come, nor height nor depth, nor any other created thing, shall be able to separate us from the love of God which is in Christ Jesus our Lord." If you ask me, spiders, heights, and going broke have nothing on being eternally separated from God. That's the most frightening thing there is, and we have an incredible assurance that God will never leave us.

The prophet Daniel could easily have succumbed to fear. Not only was he living in exile, a captive among a foreign people, he was constantly challenged for having a steadfast faith in God. His friends Shadrach, Meshach, and Abednego were thrown into a fire because they refused to bow down to idols. Daniel was thrown into a den of lions when he refused to stop praying to God.

Yet in each situation, Daniel witnessed God's miraculous deliverance. God rescued Daniel's friends from the fiery furnace, and He sent an angel to shut the hungry lions' mouths. After each of Daniel's trials, he received promotion and was able to prove that the God of Israel was all-powerful. As I studied the prophet's life, I found myself captivated by one particular passage, and I believe it helps explain why we saw the Lord move so mightily in Daniel's life.

> With flattery he will corrupt those who have violated the covenant, but the people who know their God will firmly resist him.
>
> —DANIEL 11:32, NIV

The word *know* here represents a close, warm, and even passionate intimacy coupled with the ability to process information cognitively. This combination of passionate intimacy and knowledge produces a spiritual phenomenon in a person's life. It enables us to trust God and to perceive what He is doing in our lives at the same time. This intimate relationship with God forms the very foundation of a true willingness to submit to His sovereignty in our lives and to trust that He has everything that concerns us in His hand. The people who know their God don't fear the world and the trappings of sin. They know that God is omniscient, omnipresent, and omnipotent.

I called a mentor of mine, Dr. Ray H. Hughes, to gain further insight into this passage. Although I love to study Scripture from the New International Version or *The Message*, he encouraged me to read the verse in the King James Version. Boy, am I glad I did. It says, "And such as do wickedly against the covenant shall he corrupt by flatteries: but the people that do know their God shall be strong, and *do exploits*" (emphasis added).

The word *exploits* in Daniel 11:32 means "to do great things." When we pursue an intimate relationship with God, filling our minds with the knowledge of His Word, He will give us strength to face the impossible, the painful, and the fearful. He will appoint us to do great exploits. What an incredible thought. Doing great things is a part of our God-given purpose. Do not be afraid.

Stay in the Game

While attending an Atlanta Braves game recently, I was reminded of a common practice in baseball that relates to fear. When a person strikes out, it is entered in the scorebook as the letter K because the words "strike out" won't fit in the small space allotted. "What's so special about a K?" you ask. Here's what I found interesting. When the batter swings at the third pitch and misses, it is considered a strike out, and the scorekeeper enters the letter K as I just explained. But when the batter does not swing at the pitch, the strike out is entered differently. Instead of writing a traditional K, the scorekeeper marks this with a backward Я to signify that the batter did not even try. He did not go down swinging.

Was he afraid he would miss? Was he afraid to take a chance? Was he afraid to trust himself? The backward Я represents the batter's choice to simply give up and head back to the bench to watch the game. Like many of us he might have thought, "I can't take the pressure. I don't know if I'm up to it. I'm afraid to venture out. I've got too much on the line."

Don't be that batter. Stay in the game. Don't quit. Don't let fear paralyze you from action. If you give up, you will be moving backward. Our goal in life is to keep moving forward, whether it is in our role as a spouse, parent, employee, or Christian. The Lord has greater things for us than we can imagine. (See Ephesians 3:20.) He wants to see us grow and break through any fear that would hinder us from moving into the next phase of His plan for our lives. When fear creeps in on you, staring you in the face, breathing down your neck, plant your feet, square your shoulders, look it dead in the eye, and swing your bat.

That's what Queen Esther did. Esther was a beautiful young Jewish woman living in Persia during the reign of King Xerxes. When she found favor in the king's eyes, he made her his new wife, the Queen of Persia. But when Haman, the king's prime minister, hatched a plot to kill all the Jews in the empire, Esther was forced to face her greatest fear: her own death and the genocide of her people.

When Mordecai, Esther's uncle and a palace scribe, found out about Haman's plan, he begged Esther to go before the king and intercede for the Jewish people. But Esther knew that if she went before the king without being summoned, she would break the law, which was punishable by death. I've faced tough decisions before, but none that meant putting my life on the line. Despite the risk, Mordecai told Esther that she must speak to the king.

> And Mordecai told them to answer Esther: "Do not think in your heart that you will escape in the king's palace any more than all the other Jews. For if you remain completely silent at this time, relief and deliverance will arise for the Jews from another place, but you and your father's house will perish. Yet who

knows whether you have come to the kingdom for such a time as this?"

—ESTHER 4:13–14

I've faced some difficult decisions in my day, but Esther was stuck between a rock and a hard place. Consider what Mordecai was saying to her: she could face probable death by going in to the king uninvited, or she could face certain death by remaining silent. There was no easy way out for the queen. Esther decided to face her fear and trust in God. She asked that all the Jews fast and pray for three days with her, and on the third day she went to Xerxes.

To her relief, he stretched out his scepter to her and accepted her presence. I can only imagine what Esther must have been feeling as she entered Xerxes's throne room; she was literally putting her life in the king's hands. What an amazing woman and child of God Queen Esther was!

Esther's faith was rewarded when Xerxes showed favor to his queen, saving her life. After inviting her husband to a series of feasts in the company of Haman, the very man who was seeking to destroy her and her people, she revealed her secret to them. She was a Jew, a member of the very group that was facing death for their faith. In the end it was Haman who was executed, not the Jewish people.

Esther faced her fear and was used by God to stop genocide. We too must not be afraid to do what seems impossible. God is not the author of impossible! He can make a way when there is no other way. If we perish doing God's will, then we perish. It's better to die serving God than to live and spend an eternity in hell. Fear can overpower us, manipulate us, destroy us—but only if we let it. Remember, God is not the author of fear. He is the God of "in spite of," and He doesn't want us to let fear or anything else keep us from fulfilling the calling He's placed on our lives.

CHAPTER 9

In Spite of Your Faults

A good garden may have some weeds.[1]
—Thomas Fuller

THE OLDER I get, the more sympathetic I become to those who are fighting the signs of aging. Have you ever known a person, say someone moving north of sixty, who just doesn't hear as well as he once did? For some odd reason, these individuals tend to deny it. They say others are mumbling or speaking too softly. And when you confront them with the possibility that maybe the world really isn't on mute, they get angry or feel hurt. If only they'd even entertain the idea that something could be wrong with their hearing, they might be able to improve the situation and live a more satisfying life.

Of course, when I ask people to speak up, it's because they really are talking too softly. Faults are so easy to see in others but almost impossible to recognize in ourselves. In fact, very few people can recognize their own faults and limitations without some serious soul-searching. When confronted with their failings, most people deny they exist or shift the blame onto others or outside forces. Believe me, this is much easier to do than to admit your own weaknesses.

It's difficult to deal with the realization that you have limitations. Who wants to admit he might not be as smart, talented, healthy, or tough as he thinks he is? I've tried to avoid it in my own life, but my wife keeps a running list of my shortcomings, making it more and more difficult for me to deny their existence. I've learned that understanding our faults begins with humbly accepting the fact that we are all flawed to some degree. The Bible says that all have sinned and fallen short of the glory of God (Rom. 3:23). We all share this common bond.

It never ceases to amaze me that God uses deeply flawed individuals to accomplish His purposes. I'm grateful, don't get me wrong, but it still catches me by surprise. David, the anointed king, committed adultery with Bathsheba then had her husband put on the front lines of the battlefield so he would be killed (2 Sam. 11). Despite all this, God called David a man after His own heart, a man who would do all His will (Acts 13:22).

The prophet Elijah saw God send fire down from heaven to shame the prophets of Baal in 1 Kings 18, but by the next chapter he was running for his life because Queen Jezebel threatened to kill him. How quickly he forgot how powerful his God is. The God of Abraham, Isaac, and Jacob could rain down fire, stop the sun, and even turn a murderer into a martyr, but Elijah felt the need to run from a wicked queen instead of trusting God to deliver him. The apostle Paul once took delight in killing Christians, but God raised him up to become one of the most influential men in the early church.

Who but the Lord could redeem these men in the wake of such choices? I thank God for His willingness to look past our faults and see our potential. If the Lord was unwilling to do that, I don't know where I'd be.

"Chuck Missler once said, 'The amazing thing about God is that He can do anything but chooses to only do things through us.' That makes me scrutinize my own choices even more severely than I might otherwise."[2] —RICK TORBETT

LESSONS FROM THE WILDERNESS

Moses learned this the hard way. Although he walked close to the Lord, Moses was not free from faults. He recognized many of his shortcomings, but he may have been a little too self-aware. He almost let his faults keep him from fulfilling God's plan for his life.

Moses was born when the Jews were enslaved in Egypt. Pharaoh had decreed that all male Hebrew infants be drowned at birth, but Moses's mother, desperate to save her son, put her baby boy in a basket and sent him floating down the Nile River. Hearing the crying child as she walked by, Pharaoh's daughter pitied the Hebrew infant and adopted him as her own.

It surely was no coincidence that the Jews' future liberator was raised as an Egyptian prince. Had Moses grown up in slavery with his fellow Hebrews, he probably would not have developed the pride, vision, and courage to lead them out of slavery. God had a purpose for Moses from the beginning, just as He does for us.

When Moses was a prince of Egypt, he wore fine clothes, lived in a palace, and had someone attending to his every need. He was a warrior and an architect, but when he went to see about his Hebrew brethren and saw an Egyptian mistreating a slave, Moses's anger got the best of him. Moses killed the man and was forced to flee Egypt or risk being sentenced to death.

After experiencing the luxuries of Egypt, I imagine Moses experienced a dramatic dip in his self-esteem and self-confidence. He suddenly went from prince to pauper, from free man to fugitive. He didn't have the relationship with God he would later be blessed to enjoy, so he was left to sort through these strange emotions on his own.

During his forty-year exile in the desert of Midian, Moses became a simple shepherd and began raising his family. Before he challenged Pharaoh, before he led the Hebrews out of Egypt, before the Red Sea parted and God gave him the Ten Commandments, Moses was just a regular man, full of strength but also of weakness, trying to survive and carve out an existence in the Sinai Desert. When he met God at the burning bush and heard His voice, Moses was forever changed. This burning bush experience would perpetuate Moses's acceptance of his weakness and faults, and solidify in his mind that God's power was great enough to conquer those flaws.

In Exodus 3, God called Moses into His service and commanded him to deliver the children of Israel from their slavery in Egypt. Immediately Moses was faced with a situation that must have brought him much anxiety. He knew his faults. He also knew the power of Pharaoh. Remember too that Moses had a battered sense of self-worth. Look closely at this passage.

> "Now therefore, behold, the cry of the children of Israel has come to Me, and I have also seen the oppression with which the Egyptians oppress them. Come now, therefore, and I will send you to Pharaoh that you may bring My people, the children of Israel, out of Egypt." But Moses said to God, "Who am I that I should go to Pharaoh, and that I should bring the children of Israel out of Egypt?"
>
> —EXODUS 3:9–11

Moses was full of fear. He knew his faults, so he made excuses in hopes that God would see them as reason enough to find someone else for the task. All five of Moses's excuses in Exodus 3 and 4 stemmed from his insecurity, which is a form of unproductive fear. We'll consider each one because you might be surprised how often they still appear.

1. "I'm not worthy."

Moses questioned his worth before God, and the Lord's answer to Moses is the same one He gives us when we question our fitness to answer His call. God said, "I will certainly be with you" (Exod. 3:12). No matter what the obstacle, if God is with you, the odds are entirely in your favor. God plus you is always a majority.

2. "I don't know enough about God."

Oftentimes we think we need more education or experience before we can do the things God asks of us. We count ourselves out before we even get started. God gave Moses a five-word theology lesson. He said, "I AM WHO I AM" (Exod. 3:14). With those simple but profound words, God told Moses that He was the One who could do the impossible and deliver His people from captivity. And He still is.

3. "What if the people don't believe me?"

This was probably the least of God's concerns, and His response went to the real heart of the matter. Instead of sending down fire from heaven or causing a tree to miraculously shrivel up, God allowed Moses to experience His power. He told Moses to throw down his rod, and it suddenly became a serpent. Then the Lord had him reach out to pick the snake up, only to have it return to wood.

He went on to instruct Moses to put his hand inside his cloak. When he pulled it back out, it was covered with leprosy, a deadly disease. When God had Moses do the same thing again, Moses's hand returned to normal (Exod. 4:1–9). What God did for Moses here is important. He allowed him to see that He would use him to perform His mighty acts. God knew the real issue wasn't whether the people believed Moses, but whether Moses believed Him.

4. "I cannot speak in public. I'm slow to speech. I stutter."

Now remember, God had just turned Moses's rod into a snake, and yet His chosen deliverer still wasn't convinced God could overcome his weaknesses. I've been in a similar place myself, and God answered me in those times of weakness in the same way He answered Moses. "So the Lord said to him, 'Who has made man's mouth? Or who makes the mute, the deaf, the seeing, or the blind? Have not I, the Lord? Now therefore, go, and I will be with your mouth and teach you what you shall say'" (Exod. 4:11–12). Has God ever done that for you? He's given me the right response more times than I can count. In a later chapter, I'll tell you about just one of those instances.

5. "God, why don't You send somebody else?"

This was Moses's last-ditch effort to get out of a task that he felt wholly unqualified for, and God's response to Moses at this point is the most frightening of all His answers. The Bible says the Lord's anger was kindled against Moses, and He agreed to let Moses's brother Aaron speak in Moses's stead. God would give Moses the words, and Aaron would be Moses's spokesman (Exod. 4:14–16).

This was plan B, not plan A. God had every confidence that Moses could complete the task He was giving him, and Moses shortchanged himself. I never want my fears and faults to keep me from walking in the fullness of what God has for me. I take some consolation in Exodus 4:17. God told Moses that Aaron might be his mouthpiece, but "you shall take this rod in your hand, with which you shall do the signs." Despite Moses's protests, God would demonstrate His power through Moses. He refused to allow His fearful child to miss his calling.

Have you ever felt as Moses did? Maybe you are identifying with him now. I know I sure have. I felt inadequate when I began writing this book. I knew God told me to do it, but it took me years—eight years to be exact—to complete the project you are holding in your hands. How's that for procrastination?

Before writing this book, I felt inferior to complete the task and gave the Lord my own list of excuses: I was not an author. I was not a well-known speaker. I have always been a behind-the-scenes type of guy who helped the "famous" guys. What if no one is interested in what I have to say? I wanted the Lord to give this task to someone else, but I had to realize that God didn't ask me to be an acclaimed author or popular speaker. He asked me to write a book, to obey just one command. So no matter how God chooses to use this book, I know one person who will be blessed by this project—me, because I did what God asked me to do.

When faced with challenges, especially ones we feel we cannot handle, we all tend to focus on our weaknesses instead of our strengths. We have seen this on a much larger scale in recent years. Today in the United States it seems we all are facing self-esteem issues to some degree. With the collapse of the world's financial market, America is no longer the world's financial giant. Our confidence in the US economy is faltering as people lose jobs, use up their savings, and wonder if the situation will ever turn around. Industries that once were the hallmark of success are laying workers off and shutting down. One county in the state of Georgia cut more than five hundred teacher positions in one year.[3] There was a time when the idea that a teacher might be laid off because of budget constraints was simply unheard of.

Our fears are taking shape and unfolding on the evening news, and like Moses, we feel insecure. Millions affected by the weak economy have lost confidence that the situation will ever get better. Yet despite these economic realities I challenge you to remember the promises of God. Walk confidently in the Word and know that He alone is your provider. Your job is not your source; God is! Your spouse is not your source; God is! Your children are not your source; God is! Your bank account is not your source; God is!

Throughout this life, we will all have times of doubt. Like Moses, we will feel inadequate to meet God's challenge. But I believe the Lord still uses those who are willing to trust Him to do the miraculous. The Lord loves to take the obedient and give them great success. It is seldom the obvious choice God selects for greatness. Remember David? Even his own father didn't expect his ruddy young son to be God's choice for king. (See 1 Samuel 16:1–13.) But the Bible says, "The Lord does not see as man sees; for man looks at the outward appearance, but the Lord looks at the heart" (1 Sam. 16:7). The most important choice I can make on a daily basis is not how I can better lead others but how I can better lead myself. The most difficult person I will ever lead is me. Leading myself is a choice I make.[4] —SHAWN LOVEJOY

God's First Pick

One of the most heartbreaking choice processes I have ever witnessed as an educator has been on the playground. Not the first place you think of when talking about something serious, is it? Playgrounds are usually full of laughter and play, a place most kids look forward to going, but if you think all children jump for joy at the thought of spending a half-hour outdoors, you'd be wrong.

Recess can be a terrifying experience for many children. Why? I have two words for you: team sports. Surely it hasn't been that long. You remember how it works. Team captains are chosen, then each captain selects his or her teammates. If the captain really wants to win, he will try to gain an advantage by choosing the best players for his team. The weakest players are always the last to be chosen. Some captains may even choose to play with fewer team members just to avoid having these weaker players on the team. This process can crush a child's self-esteem. We all desire to feel wanted or needed. Some children are left with lasting scars when they are repeatedly the last to be chosen.

When I was a teacher, I made it a point to choose teams myself instead of leaving this up to the children. I would strategically select from the less talented group first, coupling them with a more talented person immediately. Sometimes I would number the kids, and all of the children with the same number were on the same team.

Why am I taking you back to the playground? Because this pattern of wanting only the best players and labeling people based on our perception of their value doesn't change when we become adults. As parents, we want to send our children to the best schools to give them the biggest advantage in life. At work, we want to see the best candidates hired. We want the person for the job who may give our company an advantage in the market or the candidate who can best enable the business or ministry to grow. It's recess all over again.

We all are important in God's eyes. It is His desire that we are always chosen first, that we always succeed, that we all win! In every game someone has to come in second place, but that does not reflect that person's value—spiritually or in the natural.

I believe that we as parents should be the first to display unconditional love to our children so that they can begin to understand the love of their heavenly Father at an early age. Each night I lay my hand on my daughters and pray that God will give them healthy self-esteem and cause them to see themselves as He sees them. No matter where my daughters fall in society's pecking order, I want them to know how much they are loved.

God's design is that we all feel special because in His eyes we are. We all are His first pick. No one is left off the team. In the game of life, God has equipped all of us with skills, talents, and gifts that He expects us to contribute back to society. In doing so, we fulfill His purpose for our lives and attain a sense of personal fulfillment. So the next time you are charged with choosing a team, think about everyone involved, not what it will take to win. You may never know the impact you have on those who feel unwanted.

NO MORE EXCUSES

Just like Moses, we are faced with a choice. Do we trust God, or do we give in to our self-doubt and feelings of inadequacy? Moses had to choose between giving in to unproductive fear and walking in the anointing of God. Would he return to the land that had caused him so much strife to deliver a people he barely knew? Would he risk his life and his family to answer the call of God? Moses didn't believe he could do what God was asking him to do, so he made excuses.

We know how it ended for Moses. We know of the miracles that delivered the Hebrews, God's chosen people, from Pharaoh's yoke of slavery. We can probably recite most of the plagues God sent when Pharaoh refused to let the Israelites go, and who can forget the dramatic parting of the Red Sea? Yes, despite Moses's many faults, God used him in a mighty and powerful way.

I know there are people who have the same self-esteem issues Moses had. Sometimes I don't feel adequate, but God can use anybody. He can speak through anyone, even a donkey, so the story goes. If you aren't sure what God has called you to do, ask Him to reveal it to you. If you seek the Lord, He will direct your path. You have this promise in Matthew 7:7-8: "Ask, and it will be given to you; seek, and you will find; knock, and it will be opened to you. For everyone who asks receives, and he who seeks finds, and to him who knocks it will be opened."

I believe He has greatness in store for you and me. His Word says He does. And no mater what you have done, nothing can cancel His plans for you.

CHAPTER 10

In Spite of Your Failure

Good decisions come from experience, and
experience comes from bad decisions.[1]

—Author unknown

ONE OF THE greatest duties I have here on this earth is to serve and lead my family. Being faithful to my wife and our two daughters is the greatest testament I can give to God's love and care for us. I like to think I fulfill this responsibility pretty well, but in truth, I have failed in this responsibility many times.

One instance stands out in particular. I love to get out and work in the yard. I click on my iPod and zone out. Whatever I'm thinking about fades away. It's just the grass and me. On this day, I came home from work and my then four-year-old daughter greeted me at the door, all hugs and smiles.

"Daddy, can we play?"

"Sure, baby, we can play, but Daddy's got to cut the grass first."

I changed clothes, went outside, and cranked up the lawn mower. True to form, I clicked on some tunes and focused on the grass. I wanted it to be immaculate, a yard that would be the envy of the neighborhood. I mowed evenly, smoothly, taking just the right amount of grass off the top. It was a masterpiece. I admired my work, proud of my skill and accomplishment.

When I went into the house to get a drink of water, my daughter said, "Daddy, can we play now?"

I told her, "Sure baby, just a few more minutes. I've got to trim the shrubs."

Each time I buzzed my Weed Eater past the big window on the front porch, I would look over and see my little girl with her nose pressed against the glass, staring at me, waiting patiently to play. When I finished the trimming, I went inside again to get another drink of water.

"Daddy, is it time to play now?"

"Almost, baby. I just need to blow off the driveway and porch."

Again, I left my little girl to go outside and tend to my masterpiece. While I was blowing away the lawn debris, the sun started to set. Yet when I looked up at the window, she was there, still waiting.

By the time I finished the lawn work and put all my tools away in the garage, it was dark. It was my daughters' bedtime when I went inside, but my little girl was still standing by the window, waiting on her dad to play. She was waiting for me to keep my word, to fulfill my promise. And I let her down.

You might say, "Richie, that's not that big a deal." Well, it is a very big deal to me. I messed up! Perhaps it wasn't a major catastrophe. Sure, nobody was injured, lost, or killed. But I failed to complete my primary task as a father, which is to nurture my child. It was my own personal failure, a bad choice. That night I realized that the days of my daughter wanting me to play with her, or even to be in her life, are numbered. I missed a great opportunity to connect with my child.

If we ever attempted to list our failures, it would probably take a lifetime, with new entries being added to the list each day. Amazingly, God looks beyond those failures and continues to grant us new opportunities to serve Him. Although we see the ugly past and can't always move on, He sees the future and desires greatness for all of us. All have sinned and fallen short of God's glory (Rom. 3:23), but God treats us much better than we deserve, and because of Christ Jesus He freely accepts us and sets us free from our sins.

LESSONS FROM A GIANT KILLER

Failure is the state or condition of not meeting a desirable or intended objective. It may be viewed as the opposite of success. The simple truth is that failure is one of those experiences in life that we cannot escape; it is common to all of us no matter our gender, age, experience, or beliefs. According to 1 John 1:8, "If we say that we have no sin, we deceive ourselves, and the truth is not in us."

Thus, one of the requirements of this life is that we gain the ability to handle failure in its varying degrees, moving toward a greater maturity and a deeper sense of our own spirituality. A careful study of the Bible suggests that most of the great figures of Scripture, the ones we admire and model our lives after, experienced failure at one time or another. They weren't always perfect. They didn't always make the right decisions. They didn't always have the best intentions.

However, the most beautiful and intriguing part of their life stories is that their failures did not keep them from serving God or being in communion with Him. Though they all failed, often in life-altering ways, they not only recovered from their failure, but they also used it as a tool for growth. They learned from their failure. They confessed their mistakes to God, and because of God's grace and mercy, He used them in even mightier ways for His kingdom.

"Honor isn't about making the right choices. It's about dealing with the consequences."[2] —ANONYMOUS

King David is one of my favorite characters in the Bible. A mighty warrior and prolific writer of Psalms, he is a prime example of failure and restoration. David is arguably one of the most exalted and celebrated heroes in the Bible. During his forty-year reign as the anointed ruler of Israel, he united the Israelites, led them to victory in battle, and conquered land, paving the way for his son Solomon to build the holy temple. Truly, David was an anointed king.

He began his life as a shepherd, tending his father's flocks. In order to protect the sheep he had charge over, David killed a lion and a bear with the same slingshot he used when he confronted the nine-foot, armored Philistine Goliath of Gath. After skilled warriors had cowered in fear for forty days, David made a weapon, invoked God's name, and killed the giant. How many shots did it take for David to hit Goliath? One. He had four more stones in his bag, but he only needed one to find his mark (1 Sam. 17).

After this military victory, King Saul made the young David commander of his troops. David proved himself a skilled warrior and leader, successfully defeating the Philistines in many battles. This is where David's trouble began. King Saul became jealous of David and his success, and he tried to kill David by throwing a spear at him. When he failed, the king tried to get his son Jonathan, David's close friend, to kill him (1 Sam. 18).

Saul's ploy failed, but David was not safe for long. Saul tried again to take his life, forcing David to live on the run from his king. One night, David entered a cave where Saul was sleeping, but instead of taking the life of the man who had been hunting him, David spared his life. Saul was killed a short time later, and David became king at the tender age of thirty. Professionally, David was "the man." He was a celebrated warrior and a respected leader, but his tumultuous personal life tells a very different story.

In 2 Samuel 11, the Bible tells us that one day when David stayed home from battle, he saw a beautiful woman, Bathsheba, from his rooftop at the palace. Although he discovered that she was married to Uriah the Hittite, David would not be deterred from sending for her and sleeping with her. When Bathsheba became pregnant, David recalled Uriah from battle so that he would visit his wife and the question of the baby's paternity would never be challenged. But things didn't go as David planned.

Uriah refused to go in to his wife, not wanting to indulge in comforts while his troops remained on the battlefield. Angered and panicked, David sent Uriah to the front lines of battle, where he knew he would be killed. David then married the newly widowed Bathsheba. When Nathan the prophet confronted David about the affair, Uriah's death, and his lies, David admitted his sin. In punishment, Bathsheba's child died, and David was cursed with the promise of a rebellion from within his own house (2 Sam. 11–12).

Now, remember, this is David we are talking about. He's the man, the giant killer, the poet, musician, and hero we all esteem and want to model. What happened? Greed, adultery, lies, murder—it sounds like a movie on Lifetime. Despite his long string of successes and his favor with God, David the great king had failed at life, not once but numerous times. Upon reflection, we see that David's deceptive plan worked for a time, but it broke God's heart. God despised the fact that David had sinned against Him and others (2 Sam. 12). David had failed at his relationship with God.

Can you relate to this story? Have you ever experienced a personal failure, moral failure, business failure, or relationship failure? Have you ever made a choice in your life that caused a disastrous ripple effect that seems impossible to overcome? Have you, like David, wanted to do right by God, and yet your choices left you feeling separated from God? I know I have. If we were to be honest with ourselves, we'd all admit that we've failed ourselves, our loved ones, and even God in some way. We've all fallen short of His glory.

But David's story goes on despite his failure. The king humbled himself and chose to repent of his sin. He cried out to God for forgiveness. Many of the most popular passages in the Book of Psalms are moments when David is crying out in pain and relentlessly pursuing communion with God. One example is found in Psalm 51:

> Create in me a clean heart, O God, and renew a steadfast spirit within me. Do not cast me away from Your presence, and do not take Your Holy Spirit from me. Restore to me the joy of Your salvation, and uphold me by Your generous Spirit. Then I will teach transgressors Your ways, and sinners shall be converted to You.
>
> —PSALM 51:10–12

After he poured his heart out, David received God's forgiveness. The Lord continued to bless his kingdom and his family, even allowing the son later born to Bathsheba to become king after David's death. What a picture of restoration.

It's Not Too Late

Our stories can go on as well. It doesn't matter how miserably we have failed. We can repent, and God will always take us back. I can't find one documented time when God did not accept one of His children back when he confessed his failure. God has never turned anyone away. Our failures don't have to define our lives. God can use us, bless us, deliver us, and prosper us despite our failures, if only we ask for His forgiveness and commit to living a life pleasing in His sight.

In the end, we know David as the man who danced before the Lord, a man after God's own heart. Despite what David said and didn't say, what he did and did not do, where he went and did not go, God was the Lord of David's life. He is the God of our lives too.

We will all fail from time to time, even John Smoltz, whom we met earlier. He is now considered one of the greatest pitchers in baseball history, a future Hall of Famer, but John recounts that the best times in his career, the times when he learned the most, were the times when he failed. Don't let failure scare you. As John once told me, "I can't let a poor pitch or a loss in a game determine my self-worth as a pitcher. So I can't let a failure in my life define my whole existence. God forgets our failures; we need to do the same."[3]

I'm grateful that my brother, Eddie, learned this truth. After years of wanting to move to Los Angeles, Eddie finally saw his dream come to fruition when he spent a year living at the LA Dream Center. Under Pastor Matthew Barnett's leadership, the Dream Center ministers to countless people who are homeless or addicted or simply need to make a fresh start. For my brother, the Dream Center is where he came to realize how amazing God's grace is.

Eddie often called and wrote us, filled with excitement about God's love for him. He was learning that he could truly leave his past behind. He was learning that his past was not permanent and he did not have to be shackled by it. I thank God for Eddie's time at the Dream Center because I truly believe it was a turning point in his life. Eddie's time in Los Angeles taught him that God accepted him even when others were not as welcoming. He came to understand what we all must learn—that God looks beyond our faults and sees our needs.

Keeping the baggage from the past prohibits us from moving on to what God has in store for our future. Don't allow the enemy to steal your "mind time" by having you dwell on unfruitful thoughts. Your past is over. In Christ, all things are made new. Understand that when you fall into sin, you have an Advocate in the Holy Spirit

(1 John 2:1). He will plead your case before the Father, who longs to restore you just as He restored David. When you fail—and you will—I would challenge you to get up, dust yourself off, and run back to the cross, because that is where He will be waiting for you.

CHAPTER 11

In Spite of Your Faithlessness

When you have come to the edge of all light that
you know and are about to drop off into the
darkness of the unknown, faith is knowing one of
two things will happen: there will be something
solid to stand on or you will be taught to fly.[1]

—Patrick Overton

I DREAD THE DAY my girls reach the age of sixteen, but it's not for the reason you think. I've accepted the fact that my daughters will one day start dating, and I imagine I will have to suffer a long line of teenage boys vying for their time and affection. No, dating is not what scares me about my girls turning sixteen.

I am afraid of the day when my beautiful daughters will walk into the den, find me sitting with my feet propped up, watching the NBA Finals, and ask for the keys to the car. Boys I can handle, but turning over my keys will require great faith. I know I'm not alone; any fathers out there with me?

Walking by faith is so challenging because it requires us to relinquish control. When I hand my daughters the keys to the car, I will have to trust their ability to manage the automobile—and God's ability to protect them from everyone else on the road! The same is true in our walk with the Lord. Faith is total trust in God, often when we can't see what's ahead of us, how God will work things out, or what He is doing in our lives. I admit, I've tried to help God out a few times, and it never works. Faith is a matter of trusting Him with the outcome.

Throughout Scripture, there are numerous examples of God calling on His people to exercise faith. Abraham was ninety-nine years old when God told him his ninety-year-old wife, Sarah, would conceive and bear him a son. Sarah laughed out loud at the idea of it. They had waited so long for God to fulfill His promise to make Abraham's descendants as numerous as the stars in the heavens Sarah tried to bring God's Word to pass herself. Desperate to be a mother, Sarah sent her maidservant in to sleep with her husband. Hagar gave birth to a son named Ishmael, but the child's presence created so much friction between the two women that eventually Hagar was sent away. Does that sound familiar? Abraham's grandson Jacob would eventually experience a similar dispute between his wife and her maidservant.

In order for Abraham to have faith in God, he had to believe God's promise. There was no other option. Either God was true, and Abraham would be the father of many nations, or He was a liar. In Genesis 21, we see the fulfillment of that promise:

> And the LORD visited Sarah as He had said, and the LORD did for Sarah as He had spoken. For Sarah conceived and bore Abraham a son in his old age, at the set time of which God had spoken to him. And Abraham called the name of his son who was born to him—whom Sarah bore to him—Isaac.
>
> —GENESIS 21:1–3

The Bible says Sarah conceived "at the set time of which God had spoken to him." God has a specific time to bring about His will, but He doesn't always reveal that time to us. Yet not waiting on the Lord can lead to heartache. The son Hagar bore also had many descendants. Unfortunately, to this day Ishmael's children, broadly viewed as the Arab people, are still at odds with Isaac's descendants, the Jews. The tension in the Middle East stems back to an elderly couple who grew impatient for the promise.

CPUs, ROIs, and Other Foreign Phrases

Webster's dictionary defines *faith* as confidence or trust in a person or thing, a belief that is not based on proof. Regardless of our cultural backgrounds or our upbringing, we have all been told in some way to "keep the faith" or that we "have to have faith." Faith is used in a multiplicity of ways, but the interesting thing about the word is that in almost every usage, it has a positive connotation. As long as we keep the faith or don't lose our faith, the expectation is that everything will work out.

I think back to when I first came to work as an executive pastor at a large church in Georgia. In college I had majored in business, studying subjects such as economics, accounting, and marketing. But eventually I changed major programs and ended up with a degree in education. Why? I found accounting class to be incredibly boring, especially at 8:00 a.m. The switch was cinched when I spent all night riding the bus back to campus after playing an away basketball game. I arrived home at 5:00 a.m. and wanted desperately to sleep, but I couldn't rest because I had to make it to class in just a few of hours. Right then and there I decided that a business degree just wasn't worth losing sleep. Education classes didn't start until later in the morning.

I am so thankful God used that 8:00 a.m. class to change the course of my life. I absolutely loved every day I spent pouring into the lives of young men and women as an educator. It became a ministry for me, and it truly was my passion. More importantly, the decision to change my major moved me to the city in Georgia where I met my wife. That one decision started the amazing journey I am still on today.

After graduating with my degree in education, I pursued a graduate degree in administration and supervision. I spent the next fifteen years speaking the language of an educator. When I went to meetings, we would talk about

SATs, ACTs, CRCTs, ERBs, MATs, and GREs. I was good with the lingo and felt confident speaking that language. I had great faith in my training and ability in that arena.

However, after I became a church administrator, my confidence level changed. When I walked into my first big business meeting at the church, I realized that the tables were turned. Because I knew the Lord had called me to this position, I said, "OK, Lord. I'm going to be obedient and I'm going to do this, but I'm not really trained in this position." It didn't take long for me to realize I was a little out of my element.

My head was spinning from the plethora of new business buzzwords that had developed in the fifteen years I was busy in education. Imagine my frustration when the guy I was meeting with said, "Your S-U-M will be determined by your C-P-Us, and that will provide a greater R-O-I."

"Whoa!" I thought. "What was that?"

During that first meeting, whenever we discussed something I was unfamiliar with, I wrote everything down. Some concepts made me think, "Oh, I think I remember what that means," while others were more like a foreign language. A group visiting for that first meeting made a well-prepared, informative presentation, and like any good minister who needs to buy himself some time, I replied to their presentation by saying, "You know what? I'm going to pray about it, and I'll get back to you tomorrow with our decision." That was all I knew to say when I realized I was way over my head, and boy did I ever have a conversation with God!

I complained all the way home. "God, I can't believe You put me in that position. How could You do that to me? You know I don't know what they're talking about. I looked like an idiot. You humiliated me in front of everybody. You told me it was going to be OK if I went to work at the church. I was just fine working at the school, doing what I was trained to do, and You put me in that position to fail."

Well, thank God for Google! I went online and looked up CPUs and ROIs, pulling an old-fashioned all-nighter. I had been charged with running the church business, and I believe business is still business. The church wanted the best deal. We always took three quotes for a job, just as all businesses do. The church deserves discounts, points, and so on for the good of the congregation. Those of us handling church funds need to be good stewards of the money the congregation gives.

So we closed the business deal, but unfortunately I had just a little meanness inside of me. I thought about all those letters in their presentation, and I wanted to say, "You know what? Your proforma better do what it says with all your CPUs and your ROIs, because if you don't, you're going to L-O-S-E this J-O-B, and your K-I-D-S may not E-A-T." Don't worry. I kept those thoughts to myself. Although I knew I had been called to this position at the church, my faith wavered when I was challenged with concepts that were unfamiliar to me.

We all experience challenges to what we have faith in, but if we can trust, repent, and believe, God will always come through. My path shifted from education to full-time ministry, and this directed me into opportunities I never could have imagined. God is continually blowing my mind with new ways He is expanding my ministry. Never underestimate the potential of what God can do with what may seem like an insignificant choice. God makes the insignificant significant. I am a living testimony to this!

"Dreams don't require talent; they require choices."[2]—CHRIS SONKSEN

TRUST, REPENT, AND BELIEVE

I cannot think about the issue of faith without reflecting on the story of Simon Peter. Now, he was my kind of guy. One of Christ's twelve disciples, and one of three who were especially close to Christ, Peter had an aggressive personality. He was a roaring lion, a real go-getter.

Peter was the kind of man who would have blitzed the quarterback every play or tried to hit a home run every time he walked up to the plate. Peter had a competitive spirit; he was passionate in everything he thought, felt, and did. There was no halfway mark for him. It was all or nothing with Peter. He was so passionate about his faith in Christ that he forsook all to lead others to Him. But he was not perfect.

In fact, Peter struggled with his faith. He doubted, he wavered, and he compromised before he learned to stand firm in his faith and in the truth. Throughout Scripture the story of Peter demonstrates, in my opinion, one of the finest examples of a faith journey. In Peter, we can see faith at its strongest and faith at its weakest. Only a few moments separate the ultimate example of mountain-moving confidence in God and a total lack of trust in Christ.

> Now in the fourth watch of the night Jesus went to them, walking on the sea. And when the disciples saw Him walking on the sea, they were troubled, saying, "It is a ghost!" And they cried out for fear.
>
> But immediately Jesus spoke to them, saying, "Be of good cheer! It is I; do not be afraid." And Peter answered Him and said, "Lord, if it is You, command me to come to You on the water."
>
> So He said, "Come." And when Peter had come down out of the boat, he walked on the water to go to Jesus. But when he saw that the wind was boisterous, he was afraid; and beginning to sink he cried out, saying, "Lord, save me!" And immediately Jesus stretched out His hand and caught him, and said to him, "O you of little faith, why did you doubt?"
> —Matthew 14:25–31

Peter not only witnessed a miracle, but he also trusted Jesus, putting all his faith in Him. He got out of the boat. I think that's amazing. He walked on water. I don't know whether or not I would have had the courage to do what Peter did. But then, for just a moment, he took his eyes off Christ. He doubted. He wavered. He sunk. Peter didn't have the faith to go the distance, at least not yet.

Peter lost his faith more than once during his life. Even though he met daily with Jesus—ate meals with Him, witnessed His healings and miracles, and pledged his allegiance to Christ—he did the very thing he said he would never do when he denied Jesus not once but three times.

> Then Jesus said to them, "All of you will be made to stumble because of Me this night, for it is written: 'I will strike the Shepherd, and the sheep of the flock will be scattered.' But after I have been raised, I will go before you to Galilee." Peter answered and said to Him, "Even if all are made to stumble because of You, I will never be made to stumble." Jesus said to him, "Assuredly, I say to you that this night, before the rooster crows, you will deny Me three times." Peter said to Him, "Even if I have to die with You, I will not deny You!" And so said all the disciples.
>
> —Matthew 26:31–35

Later that night after being with Christ in the Garden of Gethsemane and witnessing His arrest and trial, Peter lost his faith. Just as he had done before, Peter took his eyes off Jesus. Each time Peter rejected Christ, the denial was more emphatic than the one before.

> Now Peter sat outside in the courtyard. And a servant girl came to him, saying, "You also were with Jesus of Galilee." But he denied it before them all, saying, "I do not know what you are saying."
>
> And when he had gone out to the gateway, another girl saw him and said to those who were there, "This fellow also was with Jesus of Nazareth." But again he denied with an oath, "I do not know the Man!"
>
> And a little later those who stood by came up and said to Peter, "Surely you also are one of them, for your speech betrays you." Then he began to curse and swear, saying, "I do not know the Man!"
>
> Immediately a rooster crowed. And Peter remembered the word of Jesus who had said to him, "Before the rooster crows, you will deny Me three times." So he went out and wept bitterly.
>
> —Matthew 26:69–75

But it didn't end there for Peter. Let's remember that it was Simon Peter who, on the Day of Pentecost, was called upon to preach the sermon that started the entire New Testament church. Just weeks after he denied Jesus, Peter boldly proclaimed the gospel to the very people who had participated in Jesus's crucifixion. Not only did he affirm that Jesus was the Son of God, but he also warned his listeners that if they didn't accept Him, they would face God's wrath (Acts 2). That's not exactly what I'd call subtle. Although he denied Jesus, Peter was still mightily used of God. In the same way, your purpose is not canceled because of a wavering faith.

You may remember that in the Garden of Gethsemane, Peter lashed out at the Roman soldiers arresting Jesus, literally cutting off one man's ear. But when Jesus saw what Peter had done, He simply picked up the man's ear and put it back in place. It was a miraculous healing, even if it wasn't enough to keep Jesus from going to Calvary. This happened just a few hours, a day at most, before Peter denied Christ. Peter had defended Christ vehemently only hours before he would deny knowing Him at all.

I love a point Mark Batterson makes about this moment in his book *Wild Goose Chase*. If that incident had happened in today's society, the Roman soldier likely would have sued Peter for assault and battery. He might have even accused him of attempted murder. Yet if the case *Malchus v. Peter* was tried in court, and the judge asked for proof of Malchus's claim, what would he have to show him? The ear Peter cut off would have been firmly in place and without a blemish because Jesus healed it. The judge would have no choice but to dismiss the case due to a lack of evidence! What I'm saying is this: not only did Christ heal the soldier's ear, but He also destroyed all evidence of Peter's crime. Likewise, with His sacrifice on the cross, Jesus took all the evidence, all the guilt against us as sinners and destroyed it.

GET OUT OF THE BOAT

Hebrews 11:6 says, "Without faith it is impossible to please Him, for he who comes to God must believe that He is, and that He is a rewarder of those who diligently seek Him." I want to grab hold of what's next for me. There are issues in my past that I'm not proud of; you have some too. But there are things out there that God is calling me to do, and I have to have the boldness of Peter.

I have to have the courage of Peter. I have to look past my failures, my faults, and my flaws; I have to ignore fatigue; I have to ignore fear; and I have to have the faith to accomplish what God has called me to do. As Philippians 3:13 says, "This one thing I do, forgetting those things which are behind, and reaching forth unto those things which are before" (KJV).

You do too. There are no other biblical accounts of anyone walking on water. What kind of faith must it have taken for Peter to get out of the boat? I don't know of anyone, including myself, who ever could have exhibited that type of faith without having firsthand knowledge of the omnipotence of God. We should all take a lesson from Simon Peter.

CHAPTER 12

How Can I Trust God When I Don't Understand?

In Matthew 9:29, Jesus uses the phrase, "according to your faith it will be done to you." This means you get to choose how much God is going to bless your life. It's according to your faith.[1]

—David Chrzan

J ob was minding his own business and doing incredibly well. He was like so many Christians—doing the right thing, working hard, raising his family. Job loved the Lord. In fact, the Bible calls him the greatest of all the men in the east, but Satan came along and tried his best to destroy this faithful man of God.

Job literally lost it all. I mean everything. The Bible says he lost his servants, his oxen, his sheep, his camels, his sons, his daughters, his house. When the dust settled, Job had almost nothing left of his great wealth. In modern terms, we would classify this as a personal economic crash.

He lost his stocks, his dividends. He lost his bank accounts and his contracts. His economy tanked. Everything he had worked for his whole life was gone. Can you relate? Maybe you are struggling financially or even facing bankruptcy. I know that for many of us now, *financial freedom* is a foreign word.

For a time, Job regretted the fact that he was ever born, and he blamed God for his torment. He longed for his own death, but it never came. Job's account is frequently used to comfort those who are suffering, but when I think about Job I often think of this: God never told us we would not question His purpose or His motive. I've told you a lot about my brother, Eddie, but he wasn't my only sibling. Our sister, Keri, was born fifteen months after I was, and my family always considered her a gift from God. Keri had beautiful, silky light brown hair and drop-dead gorgeous brown eyes, but she was not only attractive and talented. She also possessed a mental and physical strength like few others I've ever met.

You see, at her birth, the doctor was late arriving, and the nurses desperately wanted the doctor present at the delivery. So the nurses instructed my mother to do all she could to prevent my sister from being born. Instead of pushing the baby, who was anxious to come, my mother was told to fight her body's natural instinct and to hold on to Keri until the doctor could arrive. The result of this unhealthy advice was that Keri didn't receive enough oxygen to her small brain as she fought to be born. When she was finally delivered, she was diagnosed with a condition known as birth asphyxia, which caused her to become developmentally disabled.

As Keri got older, she also developed epilepsy. Physicians prescribed various medications in an attempt to control my sister's grand mal seizures, which were severe and came with absolutely no warning. She would experience total blackouts, causing her to drop to the floor immediately with nothing to break her fall. Because of this, Keri had her fair share of bloody noses, facial stitches, and knocked-out teeth as a kid.

No medication could control the illness, and no medical professional had an answer. My parents took Keri to every leading medical facility at the time. No one could help my sister. So my parents accepted the reality that their daughter would be developmentally challenged and suffer grand mal seizures for the rest of her life. She attended public school under the special needs program, but it soon became apparent that she was not functioning as well as some of the others.

With the frequency of Keri's seizures, it was in everyone's best interest for her to enter a specialized program. As we all knew she would, Keri excelled in the special programs. She quickly gained influence and was well liked. My sister was loving and quick to smile, but she also was fiercely competitive, a characteristic that took her to the top most often.

One of Keri's favorite activities was participating in the

Special Olympics each spring. She competed in the broad jump and softball throw and won the blue ribbon in both events several years in a row. However, one year something funny happened. Keri did not win first place in her events. It was obvious to everyone, myself included, that she was not performing at 100 percent, and as a result she earned a red ribbon for second place and a white ribbon for third place in her respective events.

When I asked Keri why she didn't do her best (as big brothers are supposed to do), her answer shocked me. She said plainly and with great resolve that she had decided that she had enough blue ribbons. She wanted some other colors. So she had strategically jumped the perfect distance for second place, garnering the red ribbon. After that, she decided she wanted a white ribbon. So she figured out how far to throw the softball in order to receive third place, ensuring that she would receive the ribbon in the color of her choice. Her strategy didn't make any sense to me. As you know, I always want to win. But Keri just wanted to add to her ribbon collection.

As time went on, Keri continued to battle her health. She began to spend extended periods of time in hospitals as her condition worsened. One fateful morning, my mother walked into Keri's room at home and found her unconscious. Keri had suffered a horrific seizure. Our mother called 911 and then watched the emergency personnel carry her daughter's lifeless body out of the house and into the ambulance. At the hospital, doctors resuscitated her body, and we all sat by the oxygen machine watching it inflate Keri's lungs. It was almost unbearable to hold my sister's hand and listen as the doctor told my family that Keri would never recover. She didn't even survive the next forty-eight hours.

At the tender age of thirty-two, my brave sister lost her life as a result of a significant seizure. My parents, my brother, and I had to make a choice the day Keri died. Do we go on with life? Do we shut down?

I can't deny that I have my fair share of questions for God when I get to heaven. I don't understand why I'm the oldest of three children and the only one still alive. I don't get that at all. I don't understand why my sister passed away at age thirty-two and my brother at age twenty-eight. As hard as I've tried, I can't comprehend why my brother made the choices he did or why he had to pay for those choices with his life. I don't understand why my beautiful and talented sister spent her whole life heavily medicated to control her severe seizures. She could not even enjoy the simple pleasures of life. I just don't get it. I don't think I'll understand why my siblings had to endure so much heartache until that glorious day when I meet Jesus face-to-face.

I take comfort in knowing this: God did not call us to understand. He didn't tell Job, "I want you to comprehend this, so I'm going to chart a path out for you and explain exactly why you've lost everything." In the same way He didn't tell the American people why He allowed the economy to face such tough times. Nor did He have a town hall meeting with those who lost loved ones in the recent earthquakes to explain why those tragic events happened. What He did say was this: "Trust in the LORD with all your heart, and lean not on your own understanding; in all your ways acknowledge Him, and He shall direct your paths" (Prov. 3:5–6).

GOD IS IN CONTROL

Trusting God despite our circumstances, despite the fact that we don't understand His purpose or His ways, will prove again and again to be one of the most difficult challenges we will face as believers. God deserves our trust, yet it is often the thing we cannot or will not give up to our Creator. In my own life recently I have been tested on the trust issue.

In 2010, our family relocated to Tennessee after twenty-two years in Georgia. A whirlwind turn of events prompted our move. It was hard to imagine embarking on any change that dramatic let alone one that would cause my daughters, who were eleven and nine at the time, to leave the only church and school they had ever known. Yet though we were all somewhat resistant to the transition at first, God made it very clear that we needed to take a step of faith. We needed to trust Him.

Because God had proven through a series of events that this move was His will for our lives, we set out on the journey to Tennessee with some confidence. I would be lying, however, if I told you I had no anxiety about taking such a big step. I was filled with great apprehension. I didn't know if my family would be happy, if we were really doing the right thing. I believed I had heard from God, but still I had my doubts. Had I seen His hand directing us, or was I misreading a series of unrelated events?

These questions plagued me as we packed boxes and loaded up for the move. I had grown up in the city we were moving to and thought this would be reassuring to both my wife and daughters. I hoped that knowing at least some of the people in our new town would help us all with our transition, but that did not put my mind at ease. I was most concerned for my oldest daughter. She was the one most resistant to the change. She was comfortable in Georgia. She had carved out a place for herself there, and she was scared of starting over in a brand-new place.

When my wife and I prayed for our oldest child, we asked God to provide for her in some very specific ways. We asked Him to give her teachers we were familiar with and to allow her to have physical education for her elective class because she enjoys athletics and excels in that area. We even asked that she be placed in a classroom in a certain part of the building with a certain group of peers and teachers, just because we knew it would make her most comfortable. We had high hopes that she would have the opportunity to be in at least one class with some of the girls she had met at a basketball camp earlier in the summer.

In total, we made ten specific requests and believed

God would give us the things we desired. After all, God loves our little girl even more than we do. So did He answer right away and respond affirmatively to every request we made? No. We went zero for ten in answers to our requests. We couldn't believe it.

Where was God? Why hadn't He come through? Didn't He know how tough this was for our girl?

Open house and orientation at our daughter's new school were gut wrenching. If it was that hard for me, I can only imagine what my daughter was feeling. She was assigned to classes with no familiar teachers, no peers she knew, and they were in the wrong part of the building. And to top it all off, she was given a bottom locker. This is a really big deal for those of you who might have forgotten what middle school was like.

My wife and I thought things were just about as bad as they could be for our daughter, but as it turned out, the situation could get worse. The one class she really wanted, the one that truly meant something to her, was not on her schedule. My daughter the athlete wasn't even given a PE class. Instead, she was assigned a math honors class due to her high test scores. Believe me, the honors part of this deal was great to me as a parent, but sixth-grade math is already so far over my head I knew I was going to be no help in the homework department.

What was God doing? What was He thinking? Did our prayers not matter to Him?

These are times when you have to dig deep—real deep.

The fact that you don't think God has heard your prayer or that He cares for you doesn't mean He is not present in your situation working things out for your good. The fact that He didn't answer your prayers in the way or in the timing you imagined doesn't mean He is not in control. When it looks like all is lost, that's when trust really matters. God never turns His back on us.

The irony of this situation is that my daughter was able to overcome these disappointments even though her parents struggled mightily. God gave her all she needed to not only survive the transition but also to thrive throughout it. Her placement in school forced her to meet new people, try different things, and prove her ability to unfamiliar teachers in areas that she may not enjoy but needs for success in life. My daughter got involved in cross-country running, a sport she had never heard of before our move, and she excelled at it. She made new friends who will one day be closer to her than those she left behind in Georgia.

"Everything can be taken from a man but
one thing: the last of human freedoms—to
choose one's attitude in any given set of
circumstances."[2] —VIKTOR FRANKL

God's will is not our will, and He proved that to me yet again in the way He answered our prayers for our daughter. The paths we would have selected for her were not His choices for her, and the same is often true in our lives. God's will for us doesn't always match our desires for ourselves.

If you're wondering how our younger daughter adjusted to the move, I'm happy to report that two weeks into her first year at a new school, when she knew no other children or teachers, she was voted Student of the Month. We were thrilled that God gave her this boost for her confidence and helped make her transition that much easier.

Never doubt that God is in control. All we have to do is trust Him. Later in the story of Job, God's faithful servant repented of his doubt, his complaining, and his wretchedness. He said, "I abhor myself, and repent in dust and ashes" (Job 42:6). It's not our job to understand. It's our job to trust God. He always delivers those whom He allows Satan to attack. Did you notice the word *allow* in that last sentence? God is not surprised by our circumstances. Satan cannot do anything to us that God does not permit.

You may ask, "Why would a loving God who you say has my best interest at heart allow me to suffer?" I cannot answer for your situation, but I will tell you that as I look back on the unpleasant events in my life, I have grown from every one of them. The intimacy in my relationship with the Lord increases. I have learned to trust God more, and my faith has flourished. I would not trade those times now for anything this world has to offer me.

I have also learned that when I go through an attack, I must be on the right track for what God has for me. A life lived in pursuit of God will not come without its trials, and if you are under attack it is because you and/or your plans are a threat to Satan. The enemy wants to attack those he considers to be dangerous. If you are a child of God, you have been chosen and bought with a price. You have been called, and you have a purpose in God's kingdom. Because of this, you will have to fight battles daily. In the face of these challenges, your faith may falter. Press on! These are the very times when you must choose to trust in your Creator, your very present help in times of trouble. Remember these two things:

1. God never gives us more than we can handle.

2. God always delivers those whom He allows Satan to attack.

No one and nothing can compare to God. I have experienced job transitions. I have buried my younger sister and my baby brother, and I can tell you without hesitation that God has always provided the strength to get me through whatever I have faced. Please do not misunderstand me. Going through trials is not fun, and I do not enjoy it, but God is faithful and loving. He has never forsaken me, and He will not forsake you! As Isaiah 40:25 declares, truly the Lord has no equal.

DOUBLE FOR THE TROUBLE

How did it end for Job? He was blessed and received double of everything he had lost. *Double.* I believe in these times of economic confusion and uncertainty that those who are steadfast in faith will be blessed in return. God will prove His faithfulness. I am praying and claiming double for my family and yours. I believe God wants to give you back everything you have lost, just as He did for Job. I encourage you to stop right now, be bold, and ask God to prove Himself faithful and bring restoration to your house. The righteous will never be forsaken (Ps. 37:28).

To drive this point home, I'd like you to indulge me for a second and say your name aloud, just your first name. You don't have to yell it. Everyone has a name, and depending on your cultural background or nation of origin, you may have three names that each help identify you in some way. You may have been named after a beloved friend or relative, and if you're like most people, your last name identifies the family you were born into (for better or worse, that's one thing in life you don't get to choose).

God has more than one name too. In fact, there are 264 names for God in the Bible, and each one identifies a different attribute about Him. He is Elohim, the eternal Creator; Jehovah Jireh, the God who provides; Jehovah Rapha, the Lord our healer; Jehovah Shalom, the Lord who is peace; and Jehovah Shammah, the God who is there, just to name a few.

Just as we answer to our name when we are called, God answers to His. So I encourage you to begin to speak His names out loud as part of your prayer time. Why? No, God doesn't need us to remind Him of who He is, but *we* need to know His names. We need to be reminded daily of God's strength and character, of His greatness and awesome power. We need to know without a doubt that this incredible God is Jehovah Nissi, the One who declares victory; that He is Jehovah Roi, the great Shepherd who watches over and takes care of us.

Hebrews 4:12 says God's Word is "living and active. Sharper than any double-edged sword, it penetrates even to dividing soul and spirit, joints and marrow; it judges the thoughts and attitudes of the heart" (NIV). When we speak God's Word, it goes to work, transforming us from the inside out and moving in our circumstances. When we begin to remind ourselves that God is our fortress, our deliverer, our strength, our salvation, the Most High, the incorruptible God, that truth begins to come alive in us. It is no longer words on a page but a reality in our lives. God isn't just Almighty in the lives of Daniel or Moses or David. He is Almighty in your life and mine.

When situations arise that test our faith, we can remind ourselves of the awesome God we serve.

He's omnipresent. He's everywhere.

He's omniscient. He knows all and still loves us.

He's omnipotent. He can do all things.

He's the God of all grace, the Alpha and the Omega, the beginning and the end, our loving Abba Father, Jesus the Messiah, and our soon coming King. And He is the God of "in spite of."

Conclusion

Nothing we have done is final, only eternity.
—Richie Hughes

W HEN I FINALLY walked into my brother's hospital room on November 22, 2002, I was surprised to find it packed with people. I remember thinking, "Why is there such a crowd in here?" Then it sunk in. The doctors had called in the family to be with Eddie. His condition must be dire indeed. This could be the day I had dreaded for months.

You see, unbeknownst to us, Eddie had decided he would no longer take the antiretroviral drugs. For months, we couldn't figure out why his health was deteriorating so rapidly. Despite great suffering, Eddie was determined to not take what he referred to as "all those pills." My brother became a recluse sitting in his apartment all alone most days. How could this once vibrant, talented, good-looking guy just give up?

He spent most days in his favorite recliner, which he had affectionately named "The Blessing," or in his wheelchair, which he called "Jazzy." That was just Eddie, always giving objects crazy names and playing ridiculous games only he understood. He also kept several colognes near him at all times. He wanted to smell good for the people who may stop by to visit.

The doctor treating Eddie told us that his system could not tolerate the strong medications that were necessary to delay the progression of AIDS. Eddie was having such adverse reactions to the meds that he made another life-changing choice to stop using them altogether. I couldn't help but wonder what was going on in his mind. Why wouldn't he take the medicine? I thought, "Hang in there, bro. Come on, we can do this!" But his mind was made up. He was resolved. He had chosen a different path.

In the final stages of his battle with HIV/AIDS, Eddie didn't leave his apartment at all. That was when I finally began to understand something about my brother and his actions. After Eddie hit rock bottom in his life, he came back home to his family. At home, he truly straightened out his life. He accepted God's forgiveness and asked Him to be the Lord of his life. But Eddie knew himself and his weaknesses better than we did.

One day, I had a revelation. I was reading my Bible and zeroed in on Mark 9:43.

> If your hand causes you to sin, cut it off. It is better
> for you to enter into life maimed, rather than having
> two hands, to go to hell, into the fire that shall never
> be quenched.

In a way, I believe that's what Eddie was doing. He didn't believe he had the strength to live victoriously over the temptations that once ruled his life. So he refused to put himself in any situation in which the enemy could win. Eddie gave his heart to the Lord and then simply waited for his time to be with his heavenly Father. He decided that he would sit quietly and let the disease ravage his body. It took less than a year.

As I watched this final part of my brother's journey through life, I couldn't help but think of the story of the prodigal son in Luke 15:11–32. After squandering his father's money living it up in the world, the prodigal son's life unravels. With nowhere to go, he goes back to his father's house. Upon his return, he simply wanted to be like any of the other servants in his father's house, not expecting to be treated like the son he was always intended to be. He believed he had forfeited his right to sonship because of the devastating choices he had made.

However, this rich parable tells us that his father treated him as if he were a king, fully restoring everything he had left behind. His father even threw a huge party in celebration of his beloved son's return. My parents reacted in the same way when Eddie came home. They were thrilled to have their son back. They celebrated his return and accepted him with an unconditional love that demonstrated the love of Christ. The past was the past, and Eddie was home! We all still wish our blessed days with Eddie hadn't ended so soon.

I pushed through the crowd of family who had gathered somberly in the room. When I reached my brother, I was shocked to see how the AIDS virus had ravaged his body. He looked lifeless though he was hooked up to IVs, a respirator, and numerous other beeping machines. He weighed less than 100 pounds. Open sores and large purple and black bruises covered his frail body. His normally well-manicured feet were black and swollen from the lack of blood flow to his extremities.

I leaned over his bed and whispered in his ear, "Hey, bro, I'm here." Hearing my voice, Eddie shocked everyone in the room. He raised his head and mumbled something to me, then immediately lay back down on his pillow. Those unintelligible words were the last ones my brother ever spoke. Even today, I often wonder what could have been so important that he would muster his last bit of energy to speak to me before slipping into a coma.

Maybe he said, "Richie, get all of these people out of here!" Or in classic Eddie sarcasm, maybe he said, "What's everybody looking at? You got a problem?" Perhaps he was trying to say I love you. I'll never know. My brother was never conscious again. My family and I watched as Eddie left this life and its pain and crossed over into a glorious life eternal. At his passing, the room was deathly quiet. No one moved. No one spoke. Everyone just stood there looking at Eddie, but he was no longer there.

You might think that Eddie's is a sad story, and I would agree that it certainly has its low points. My whole family suffered through this time in our lives, but our prayers were ultimately answered. You see, we prayed for years that God would bring Eddie back into a relationship with Him and with us. We would pray, "Lord, let him hit rock bottom if that's what it takes." I've since learned that you have to be careful what you pray for because you might just get it!

God answered our prayers for Eddie's return, and look at the end result. Eddie chose to live his last year in seclusion in order to protect his eternity. Throughout his adult life he made a lot of poor choices and eventually paid great consequences. But in the end he was redeemed. Today Eddie is walking on the same streets of gold as the disciples and the great men of God, all because of a single choice. He forfeited the ways of this world and is now living with Christ.

Eddie gave his heart to the Lord realizing it was the most important decision he could ever make. I have grown to empathize with what my brother must have gone through when he chose to trade his temporary life for eternal security. Eddie could have made it to Hollywood, Broadway, or some other entertainment arena and be living a life separated from God. But as the Bible says, what does it profit a man to gain the whole world and lose his soul (Matt. 16:26)? I have come to see this verse as my brother's testimony.

As a family, it was extremely hard for us to let go of Eddie, but our hope that we will one day be reunited with him gave us the strength to endure some very difficult days, months, and years. My parents did not get to choose whether they would have to bury two of their three children, but we all were able to decide whether to focus on our blessings or wallow in despair. Why didn't my brother experience a supernatural breakthrough, where all the fleshly desires he struggled with immediately vanished? Why didn't God allow him to go through his experience so that he would have a ministry to bless others with similar struggles? Why wasn't he healed? Why did all of this have to happen? These are the questions I will never have all the answers to while on this earth, but my family and I will continue to believe, trust, and thank the Lord for the peace and comfort that only He can give.

In Eddie's final hours, I wrote down some thoughts. I shared them at his memorial service and though they are random, they may help you understand my relationship with Eddie better. I would like to offer them to you now:

> He was bright, talented, and handsome, strong willed, opinionated, and outspoken. But, oh, how he made us laugh.
>
> As a young boy, he carried the church drama. His role played to perfection, we all got the message. His talents grew. He could sing. He could act. He could

take your heart with his charm. He left for New York. Our prayer: "Lord, keep him from harm." His idea of stardom never quite came. Closer to home we begged him to come. Atlanta now was his home, where he briefly turned from God. The tempter had his plan; his grip was now entrenched into my brother's mind. Satan tightened the vise. Deceived, evil celebrated. "We've got this one," they said. But, oh, how they underestimated the thousands who had prayed. Bad influence battled Proverbs 22:6, but we've always known that in the end we shall *win*.

Off to another city, this time out West, but unlike before, good surrounded him. The hand of the Lord outstretched, Eddie was now back in His grasp. So excited was he when he called cross-country. "Richie," he said, "God is so awesome!"

Receiving his Master's forgiveness, covered by the blood, back to Cleveland, Tennessee. He came for his closing act. Saved by the blood, with quite a story to tell, we were *all* so encouraged for Eddie. There would be *no hell*.

Once again, Satan, you've lost the battle. You'll never touch Eddie again. Disease has stricken, the body deteriorates, we sit and wait, his condition we all hate! He cannot talk, see, or respond. Days have passed with no form of nourishment. Just last week ole Eddie arose. One last blast for Mom's birthday, his final tribute to this old earth. In just a few hours twenty-eight years will cease. We've all said good-bye. We all crave his peace.

We'll praise the Lord, for my brother will make it home! Waiting at the gate, Keri will help show him his reward. It may not have been as he planned—no movies, no number one hits, no star on the walk of fame. But you've touched us all with your gift. Tonight we give you back—so proud we are of you. For your crown is in heaven, a place Hollywood could never depict. We will remember, each our special times. We'll gather, sing praises, pay tribute to you, my brother. For though you have moved on to the best act in the script, your memory lives on.

And, oh, how you made us laugh!

Eddie's story, Keri's story, my story, your story—they all have one thing in common. Choices. Ultimately, the choices we make for ourselves impact not only us but also everyone around us as well. And no matter where we start in life, our choices determine how we will finish. My sister was never given a choice, but she made the best of her situation. She lived a life filled with joy and laughter. My brother made the wrong choice, suffered the consequences, and ultimately made the right decision to surrender his life to Christ. Eddie chose death over life in order to have life over death—life everlasting. He chose to forfeit this temporal version of life here on earth so that he might have an everlasting perspective and experience eternal life with Jesus Christ.

We all have choices to make. Life or death. Love or hate. Freedom with Christ or bondage to sin. What will you choose?

ACKNOWLEDGMENTS

I never imagined I would write a book, but this Christian walk has been full of surprises. If I have learned anything, it is that I must be obedient to what God speaks to my heart. Everyone has gifts, talents, and experiences to share. What you are holding in your hands is my humble attempt to share mine.

This work may never have been finished without the encouragement of so many friends and family members, and the input, advice, and gifts of other talented individuals. Few can appreciate the team effort put into this book more than I do. As a coach, I know the power of collaboration, and I was blessed to have a great team. I will be forever grateful to many people, especially these:

My Lord and Savior Jesus Christ, who equips the unequipped and places important people in strategic places in all of our lives.

My wife, Stephanie. In my mind, God never created a better person. Your insight gave this book a richer perspective.

My daughters, Halle and Kaleigh, the two who give my life purpose. You will always be "my girls."

My parents, Dale and Brenda, whose guidance and example have proved invaluable to me. Throughout the challenges our family has faced, I have never seen anything but total reliance on God and unwavering faith.

Each friend who endorsed this book or contributed quotes, interviews, and suggestions. I cannot thank you enough for your tireless support.

Notes

1—You Have a Choice

1. Laura Moncur's Motivational Quotations, "Quotations by Subject: Chance," http://www.quotationspage.com/search.php3?homesearch=Nidetch (accessed April 8, 2011).

2. C. S. Lewis, *Mere Christianity* (HarperOne: HarperCollins Publishers, 2001), 92.

3. "Quotes About Decisions," QuoteGarden.com, http://www.quotegarden.com/decisions.html (accessed April 14, 2011).

2—Choices Made, Consequences Paid

1. "Alfred A. Montapert Quotes," ThinkExist.com, http://thinkexist.com/quotation/nobody_ever_did-or_ever_will-escape_the/222503.html (accessed April 8, 2011).

2. Dr. Ike Reighard, lead pastor, Piedmont Baptist Church, Marietta, GA, in discussion with the author, March 2011.

3—HIV, No Way!

1. "Richard Bach Quotes," ThinkExist.com, http://thinkexist.com/quotation/some_choices_we_live_not_only_once_but_a_thousand/143476.html (accessed April 8, 2011).

2. "Elisabeth Kubler-Ross Quotes," ThinkExist.com, http://thinkexist.com/quotation/i_believe_that_we_are_solely_responsible_for_our/13270.html (accessed April 8, 2011).

3. Richard W. Stevenson, "Magic Johnson Ends His Career Saying He Has AIDS Infection," New York Times, November 8, 1991, http://query.nytimes.com/gst/fullpage.html?res=9doce2d61739f93ba3575 2c1a967958260 (accessed April 14, 2011); "Magic Johnson Announces Retirement on November 7, 1991," YouTube, http://www.youtube.com/watch?v=iSfy4AhDDnw (accessed April 14, 2011).

4—What's Behind Our Choices?

1. "William James Quotes," ThinkExist.com, http://thinkexist.com/quotation/when_you_have_to_make_a_choice_and_don-t_make_it/227352.html (accessed April 8, 2011).

2. "Choice Quotes," ThinkExist.com, http://thinkexist.com/quotation/when_it_snows-you_have_two_choices-shovel_or_make/174122.html (accessed April 8, 2011).

3. "Elvis Presley," BeliefNet.com, http://www,beliefnet.com/Quotes/Inspiration/E/Elvis-Presley/Values-Are-Like-Fingerprints-Nobodys-Are-The-Sam.aspx (accessed April 8, 2011).

4. "Quotations About Decisions," QuoteGarden.com, http://www.quotegarden.com/decisions.html (accessed April 8, 2011).

5—THE PROCESS OF MAKING A CHOICE

1. Ron Edmondson, lead pastor, Grace Community Church, Clarksville, TN, in discussion with the author, March 2011.

2. Kurt A. Adler, "Socialist Influences on Adlerian Psychology," *Individual Psychology: Journal of Adlerian Theory, Research & Practice* 50, no. 2 (1994): 131-141; http://psycnet.apa.org/psycinfo/1994-43503-001.

3. Michael Ivens and Gerard Hughes, *The Spiritual Exercises of Saint Ignatius of Loyola* (London: Newton Printing, 2004), 11-12.

6—LESSONS FROM GOD'S WORD

1. Mark Cole, vice president, INJOY, in discussion with the author, March 2011.

2. Russ Lawson, "Suffering the Consequences," *Heartlight*, http://www.heartlight.org/articles/200609/20060907_consequences.html, (accessed April 8, 2011).

3. Rep. Kevin Brooks, Tennessee House of Representatives, in discussion with the author, March 2011.

7—IN THE VALLEY OF DECISION

1. Norman Vincent Peale, *The Power of Positive Thinking: 10 Traits for Maximum Results*, Fireside, 2003, 170.

2. "John Smoltz," MLB.com, http://mlb.mlb.com/team/player.jsp?player_id=122477); http://mlb.mlb.com/network/personalities/?id=9169996 (accessed April 8, 2011).

3. John Smoltz, former Major League Baseball pitcher, in discussion with the author, September 2010.

4. Ibid.

5. Mac Powell, lead singer, Third Day, in discussion with the author, October 2010.

8—I Am God of … "In Spite Of"

1. "Fulton Oursler Quotes," ThinkExist.com, http://thinkexist.com/quotation/many_of_us_crucify_ourselves_between_two_thieves/174882.html (accessed April 8, 2011).

2. Marc Siegel, "The Science of Fear," *New York Post*, July 13, 2008, http://www.nypost.com/p/news/opinion/books/item_2MQSvT3pl9Kzwrtca FoXCO (accessed April 6, 2011).

3. John C. Maxwell, *Developing the Leader Within You* (Nashville: Thomas Nelson, 2000), 103.

4. Katharine A. Phillips, *The Broken Mirror: Understanding and Treating Body Dysmorphic Disorder* (New York: Oxford University Press, 2009).

9—In Spite of Your Faults

1. "Thomas Fuller Quotes," ThinkExist.com, http://thinkexist.com/quotation/a_good_garden_may_have_some/157348.html (accessed April 8, 2011).

2. Rick Torbett, president, Better Basketball, Atlanta, GA, in discussion with the author, March 2011.

3. "Cobb County Schools Cut More Than 700 Jobs," April 23, 2010, WGCL-TV, CBS Atlanta, http://www.cbsatlanta.com/news/23240075/detail .html (accessed April 14, 2011).

4. Shawn Lovejoy, lead pastor, Mountain Lake Church, Cumming, GA, in discussion with the author, March 2011.

10—In Spite of Your Failure

1. "Quotes About Decisions," Quote Garden, http://www.quotegarden .com/decisions.html (accessed April 14, 2011).

2. "Consequences Quotes," ThinkExist.com, http://thinkexist.com/quotation/honor_isn-t_about_making_the_right_choices-it-s/11571.html (accessed April 8, 2011,).

3. John Smoltz, former Major League Baseball pitcher, in discussion with the author, September 2010.

11—In Spite of Your Faithlessness

1. "Patrick Overton Quotes," ThinkExist.com, http://thinkexist.com/quotation/when_you_have_come_to_the_edge_of_all_light_that/173385.html (accessed April 8, 2011).

2. Chris Sonksen, lead pastor, South Hills Church, Corona, CA, in discussion with the author, March 2011.

12—How Can I Trust God When I Don't Understand?

1. David Chrzan, executive pastor/chief of staff, Saddleback Church, in discussion with the author, March 2011.

2. "Viktor Frankl Quotes," ThinkExist.com, http://thinkexist.com/quotation/everything_can_be_taken_from_a_man_but_one_thing/173855.html (accessed April 8, 2011).

FREE NEWSLETTERS
TO HELP EMPOWER YOUR LIFE

Why subscribe today?

- ❏ **DELIVERED DIRECTLY TO YOU.** All you have to do is open your inbox and read.

- ❏ **EXCLUSIVE CONTENT.** We cover the news overlooked by the mainstream press.

- ❏ **STAY CURRENT.** Find the latest court rulings, revivals, and cultural trends.

- ❏ **UPDATE OTHERS.** Easy to forward to friends and family with the click of your mouse.

CHOOSE THE E-NEWSLETTER THAT INTERESTS YOU MOST:

- Christian news
- Daily devotionals
- Spiritual empowerment
- And much, much more

SIGN UP AT: **http://freenewsletters.charismamag.com**

8178